IN THE GREEN SHADOW ...

AND OTHER POEMS

IN THE GREEN SHADOW...

AND OTHER POEMS

P. H. Maycock

MERLIN BOOKS LTD
Braunton Devon

BY THE SAME AUTHOR:

Sandcastles in the Snow
War Diary and Selected Poetry
The Chocolate Kangaroo and other poems
Sitting Target and other poems

First published in Great Britain, 1996

British Library Cataloguing in Publication Data.
A catalogue record for this book is available from the British Library.

ISBN 0 86303 741-0

Printed in England by Merlin Books Ltd., Braunton, Devon.

Cover printed in England by Maslands Ltd., Tiverton, Devon.

CONTENTS

With love to Sui

For my life-long friends
Captain Robin Heath C.B.E., R.N. of *Sheffield* and *Renown*
and his wife Joan, these true tales of the sea.

TROIS IMAGES
The Passages And Terraces Of Debussy

The audiences in the terraces of Debussy
Are ghosts, they listen, but are deaf and mute,
Their music vanishes unheard and almost
Unseen. It cannot be repeated by ghosts,
For soon they disappear out of the mind
That made them...One, two, three of evanescence...
Beauty before birth in old silences —
Buried with the author of ideas.
Morning in the afternoon. What is known...?
Make me a reply if you remember
Any of this...of these things. "The past is fastened
Upon us". Ile wryte itte downe. Three images —
Past, present, or futurity...? Which, I wonder,
Which is the music of our...captivity?

IN THE GREEN SHADOW... *For Maureen Dufferin in Italy*
(Andante, piu tosto un poco allegretto)

I've lived in olive light, in the grape dusk
And cypress nights of Tuscany, or stilled
In that long vine, almost under the water
Of The Grand Canal, or gazed in Florence, gilded
With balcony sunburst down the morning Arno.
I've long been crushed by the Masters overhead —
The Quarry Masters of The Vatican —
With tonnage of belief and perilous painting
And revived at the Pieta of The Madonna,
Christ's body in her lap, in her young lap —
Old as wild relativity's incarnate...!
And I have lived, too, in that longed-for shadow,
Where footfalls should have lit and mine could fall,
'In the green shadow of Ferrara wall.' [1]

[1] W. B. Yeats — "The People"

RETURN TO THE APRIL PALACE

Sutton Montis and then South Cadbury —
Old village streets and suddenly — the Palace!
Where it still rules, high up on eighteen acres —
Abrupt green table, stronghold far above
The country under it. Massive, with woodland,
It stands, green tonsure overtopping all;
Its trees just into April leaf. Slowly
Black faced sheep, in nose-to-tail files appear,
Threading the lower slopes, with working dogs.
A hundred White Suffolks, neatly herded, gleaming
Round the green heights — calm order — a fine painting
They make. Their farm and Thomas a' Becket church there
Hold Tudor pastures; but full Camelot magic
Towers over Tudor, with once and future Spring.

April 1994 Somerset

THE HESITANT REFLECTION *(A Masterpiece)*

A ghost image is in the mirror before him,
Confirming the woman to the man you cannot
See, his back darkened to you, on the left.
In the dark of the painting they are both aware,
But not of us, in shadowed gallery,
Where their painting has been hanging for so long —
Not even of their painter any more.
This hearing masterpiece forgets us there;
And we know nothing of their circumstance.
The fault is ours. We are the fly on the wall.
We learn it from a mirror's prying stare —
Distorted, sensitive, reflection share —
A shadowy she, stands at his open door.
We have entered where we should not be, at all...

THE MARCHES OF DINHAM WEIR (Welsh Reflections)

There is the best kind of beauty
At Dinham Weir, at the mill race
Beside the Teme. The fishermen sit
Beneath green, faded domes of rain-
Roof — great umbrellas — at the pool,
By the chanting weir — the bright wide water
Rain-pitted. There they sit unmoving,
With the mill race above them — translated,
Surrounded by mist and green and dark
High woods. The fine old houses there
Peep down from their tree-hung gardens,
Too dignified to stare, but peeping
At them. The river sings all night
And day to the wide pool of silence,
Shining calmly, where the salmon
And trout all congregate and stay
Difficult to catch. The mill now,
Is a small and hard-to-find hotel,
In the echoing marble afternoons,
Under the castle walls, well guarded
From busy Ludlow on the hill.
It has the quiet of Clungenford
And Clun there, sitting in its sun there,
Under dark, watchful, Forest of Clun,
Where the Teme and Clun rivers are born —
Pure descent from that Welsh, proud land,
A barrier black with rain and silence.
Uninhabited great hills stand
Deep in dark thought, beyond our eyes.
And at the forests, under grey skies
The Welsh Border lies wild, a place
Lonely and old, with a blackness
Of history, of violent days.
Beyond is mountainous Arcadia,
And passion of possession, birthright,
And Britain's old warrior-poet people,
Rock-solid, original, Cymru.
They have song there, fine sweet-voiced women,
Laughter, and a strong team game — fierce in defence.

COUSIN JACKA

George Webber was my father's naval cook
On his destroyer, and after World War One,
He was such a good one that my father
Brought him ashore to be our family cook.
He had received his training at Portsmouth Barracks,
Though I remember best, the food at Plymouth
Barracks, and the pre-war masters there.
George remained with us till the last war,
When he became cook at our local hotel,
Where he had spent Elysian Saturday nights.
He had a poor head for beer — even two pints
Spread out, were more than enough for him. One night
When we all lived at Plumley, under Dartmoor,
He came home on the bus and tried to walk
Down the quarter mile drive, to reach the house
Beside the deer park and rivulet of the Plum,
But got himself involved with the upper deer park,
Amongst the rocks and mossy Dartmoor hollows;
And the Ancient British Hut Circles, there,
Due to steering trouble, or compass failure,
At the very outset of the journey,
And fell into the water under the bridge.
And everyone feared that he'd missed his last bus.
Eventually he appeared, having won through,
In a soaking, but victorious condition,
With the torch Granny had bought for those dark journeys
In the top pocket of his heavy raincoat,
Shining into the sky — and the bunch of flowers
He'd bought for her, held out in wobbly shine,
In front of him, to show him the way home.
He had run into every hedge and gate
With them, to reach the house. There wasn't a flower
Left on the bunch of stalks he was offering
And shakily presented to the mistress
Of the house, for whom he had a deep fondness.
He stood with celebration in his face
And his torch still shining on the ceiling,
And tangled short speech — "of most excellent fancy".
As children we could enter into it all.
He was a Cornishman, and we all loved him.
As children he was always on our side.

He used to speak about his "Cousin Jacka,"
Though he seemed to have no relatives at all.
Perhaps by "Cousin Jacka" he meant Cornish
People, because in Devon, folk call them this,
Or used to do, so my Grandfather told me.
It was as if, in Devon, they were considered
As foreign relatives across the Tamar.
This made me want to go and see it all,
And I found it beautiful — more wild, then,
And George was right about his Cornish people —
Friendly, hospitable and seldom drunk.
And I met St. Aubyn, he was funny!
"D'yer daance and praance in Penzaance?" he demanded
Angrily, when I mispronounced the name
Of that fine town. He was a good friend, but foreign
Too, of course, as I felt bound to tell him.
And I've been drawn to Jagos ever since,
And wandered about in Cornwall over the years,
In debt to great "Cousin Jacka" at St. Austell.[1]

[1] Dr A.L. Rowse. (Late Deputy Warden of All Souls)

TRUE CONTENT

Here's shape and verse of True Content
And pleasure well within your heart,
With love all charitably spent
That is the taking of good part.

Send no report of staining lies
To put about the city, then.
Do kindness here, in country eyes
With warm response to folk, often.

Here is the lamp of gentle truth
That reads all galaxies for men,
That I have held up in my youth
And lit about my way since then.

GOOD NEWS, PRELUDE AND GROUND *(Wm. Byrd)*

Long shadows in the fields of dawn at Advent
And voices calling to the flocks and stars
Before the world was born again in winter,
Before the world turned over and awoke
To the broad day of our deliverance.
The winter boy stirs warmly on his way —
    Love's suffering to obey.
    Our maker makes to stay,
To make our day — our everlasting day!

SID VALE, SIDFORD DEVON

Gentle slopes and golden singing,
Windows gleaming by the wood,
Cottage sunset, colour bringing
To the hills, where days were good.
How I loved, across that Vale,
To breathe the scents of evening, pale,
And see below, the light
Go early into night,
And watch the late sun still
Warm Salcombe Hill.

Dark the river flashed with spark-light,
And village lamps in glittering pool.
Then when dawn skies filled with lark light,
It made all fresh and virginal.
Dawn's shining wings spread in the sky,
It set the birds to sing and fly,
Until at last, below,
Full day began to glow,
And valley-light to fill
From Salcombe Hill.

Afternoons of blue-filled skyway
Poured their gold on green, unspoiled,
While distant cars crept up the highway —
Steep-rising turns, where some truck toiled
Its way up with good local beer —
'Fresh crabmeat' — so mouth-melting here!
The fields drank thirsty light,
And all was golden-bright,
With Paradise to spill
Down Salcombe Hill.

ARRANGING FOR A CHAT WITH THE POET TOMORROW

I drove down Tiphill out of Long Dogs Lane
To park my car in Jesu Street
Well pleased to have no rain.
I went through Sandhill, then, with idle feet
After a pull of pale at the Lamb and Flag.
I climbed up Cornhill passing Stafford House
To Paternoster Row, our Georgian crown
And turned by the vast church's bulk and down.
Sun dried, I let my footsteps lag
A little, by Donnithorne's and Raleigh House
To where the streets all meet,
Close by old brick-nogged Manor and —
Deep, cellarous, from the heat —
King's Arms and London Inn
Where I went in
To each, and took my stand;
Saying it would be silly
To go as far as Piccadilly
Lane,
With thirsty summer here again.

Tomorrow I shall go
And talk to Coleridge where his gardens grow
Across the churchyard wall:
And see the saucered fields
Rise up surrounding all
With planned and patterned yields,
That every season changes
And colour still arranges
In the same sky-made way
Of his young day-to-day.

Ottery-St-Mary 1986

THE WHITE HORSE

The raging white-maned horses of the sea
Call out to the White Horse here, in Westbury
    Under-the-Plain.
They call out again and again
Through the steeplechase night of the sky,
    In the wind and the wild rain
    Their neighing, challenging cry! —
    Stampede of faraway hooves
    Over the plains of Salisbury's bare
    Stone Age kingdom — Gate of barbaric prayer.
    But the White Horse never moves.

THE LORDS

I like the clubbable climate in the Lords,
It is kindly, experienced and human.
People come in and sit down with the clear gaze
Of agriculture, good leadership and charm,
And greet each other — friends they met last week
Out shooting with their dogs, or at the races.
Red leather seating seems more welcoming
To law and agrees with warm debate and gazing
Round to smile at colleagues — it helps good speeches.
They are more tolerant to the other place.
Without envy they shun poison-mongers, and
Give sense to a lot of cock-and-bull, much better.
They are wise and tolerant to opposition;
And after good meals, more easy and amusing.

FROM SONGS OUT OF THE OLD SEA

I write for the young — the new
With only a few years told.
    I write for the old
Who never heard the cry,
    Or never came to be.
I write for the lovers, who
Met in the rage of their days
    And went their own ways
    Crying out to be free
As the waves are, that never tire.
But the chorus of waves reply —
"Cold freedom cries out for a fire
The blazing attraction it brings.
Give us desire with its wings!"
The sea spills onto the beach
As if it could know desire —
"Oh my dear lad! Oh my dear love!" — a sigh
As if it had heard or read
    The same anguish of speech,
And grieved from its own cold bed...

II

The sea has a measure
Continuous, remote
And without any rhyme,
But a cadent surge
Of rhythm in the night,
An overriding time,
A counterpoint of pleasure.
There's hardly a line you can quote
And all its verses merge —
Mad symbols, calm delight,
And a comforting, sad purge
Of its angry, bullying shout,
    Onto the long shore.
    And it offers nothing more.

III

The sea's words can be read
You can sort out the telling
If you wake from sleep to hear,
With its rhythm in your head.
Through the sighing prescient maze
Of talk the cold waves send,
You catch the deep sense, dwelling.
"She cries aloud" it says,
"Oh my good lad! — my dear!
But she cries it out in vain…
Whoever it may be!"
From the deep's embracing pain,
These are the words of the sea
    That never have an end.

THE TURNER

We drove across London, one day, to have a search
In the little East End junk shops for antiques.
You could still find good things amongst the jumble
Of articles spread about, in old dark rooms,
Bought from some home, in a house clearance contract,
Due to the death or departure of the owner.
The relatives dealt with a house contents man
Who took away all the unwanted items,
Or the owner sold them, before he sold the house.
We had been to quite a few, at last we came
To Manor Park and we were going no further.
It was a late afternoon of winter sunshine.
We chose a very small shop for our last call,
And could hardly see inside, it was so dark —
A very down-market junk establishment.
There were broken pictures all over the floor.
I've never seen such debris before, or again,
It was ankle-deep and completely wall-to-wall —
Unremarkable rubbish of every sort.
We walked in off the pavement, my wife and I
And just made out the owner, in his old shirt,
Across a depressing dust-hung darkness,
Sitting in a chair with most of its legs intact.
There was no counter, no shelves, simply the floor.
The whole place smelt of ancient grubby dust.
I greeted him and we peered about us
There was nowhere much to walk, in that dark box,
But as so much was broken, it hardly mattered,
Everything so "as found" as to be unwanted,
And the owner was friendly, but indifferent.
It was enough to put most people off.
I reached down despondently, to pull at a corner
Of a wooden frame, and saw the print
It contained, was still intact, the glass unbroken,
And just about holding together, as I pulled it.
We hadn't found much that day, it seemed worthwhile
At least it was sizable, old, and in one piece.
I lifted it up to take a closer look,
Rusty nails ran about inside the glass,
Over the old brown print and it was mounted.
I took it to better light, not very keen.

Across the mount at the bottom, clearly in pencil,
Was a signature — "J.M.W. Turner". We were in a hurry.
It was a Turner print of a seascape.
I smiled. Somebody, perhaps this man, himself,
Had signed it in pencil, where the frame was undone.
People sometimes did this to make a print
More saleable, and I held it up to him
Almost in joke. "How much d'you want for this
Masterpiece?" "Thirty bob, guv'nor" he said,
Also smiling — "I'll give you a quid?" — "O.K".
And the last deal was done. It was getting dusk,
The rush hour was approaching — time to go.
The traffic was beginning to growl, staccato fashion,
As it thickened up. We had to cross London
Again, for a quick cup of tea in Acton,
On our way home to Surrey. I pushed the picture
Into the back of the car. A fruitless day,
Tiring, without anything like a "find".
But we'd enjoyed ourselves, though just out hunting.
I parked by the café in the dark, in the Vale,
At Acton, near a dim street light. Then the café
Door opened, as we got out, and bright light shone
Into the back of the car, onto the picture.
It had come alive! It was unbelievable!
I stood in darkness, my hand on the car door…
Half-shut, arrested, with that weird tingling
One gets, so seldom, in life, as a collector,
At being in touch with glory. There were those clouds! —
Those luminous curves — violent racehorse curves,
Raging — a wild sea scene — a boiling harbour…
I stood, unmoving, peering in at it.
It was not a print! It was a sepia painting!
Then it went dark as the café door was shut.
I took it carefully out of the car — this painting,
Under the street lamp. Truly it *was* a Turner! —
One of his "Liber Studiorum" cartoons,
In sepia watercolour, wildly perfect,
For his series of the Channel Ports
In oils, and this was Calais, in a fierce gale.
The rusty nails slithered about in it,
Under the glass, under the light of the lamp.
A breeze blew rain, but my mind was absolutely
Enthralled and taken up with masterpiece.

I had recovered it from a rubbish dump,
Glory! — part of a great artist — his work
Was in my hands! I owned it for a pound —
A magic, lovely thing — unmatchable!
The storm roared in the picture and in my mind.
Sui called to me — "aren't you coming in? —
What's the matter?" "Look!" I shouted, "just look!"
And we stood there, under the Acton lamplight,
In blustery winter raindrops, staring at it —
Looking at raving, shining, damaging sea,
And the Turner, in clouds racing over it all —
Calais and shipping huddled against storm fury!

THE BIRD IN THE SHELL

There is a singing reality around us,
A brilliant city standing out of our senses,
Rising beyond material, in truth,
Not within touch of your bald entelechies,
But smiling, golden and fine, beyond our shell.
    We must peck our way into day
        And join the song.

A CURE FOR INFLUENZA

My poetry sings for me to other people.
    I don't want anything else.
        I don't compete at all.
One old lady wrote to me and thanked me —
I had cured her of 'flu. She was delighted
With my poems! Her friend had sent her
"The Chocolate Kangaroo" when she was in bed.
She said it cured her. She got up. What else? —
        She sent me her own.

SOUTH AFRICA 1942

At Wineberg, with Nicky Loew, and Abe Bailey's daughter,
Near Retreat, up-country from Capetown, the best
Land for a great vineyard — Dutch Colonial
House, stone built, with its toffee-golden woodwork,
And bee's-waxed floors and an exquisite garden.
There were prisoners, in colourful shirts, blue-trousered.
They included murderers, with life in prison —
Life jail! The sentence was death to tribal blacks!
Who sickened and died so soon, in a cell. They spent
Their peaceful lives as gardeners, round Nicky's
Vineyard House, with some pay. We rode his horses
Round the estate. He had a framed document
In his hall, an original warrant signed,
For the execution of King Charles the First.

BEFORE CHRISTMAS

The sea shares truth with me
As I listen for its message,
As I lie at night, in bed
With Advent in my head,
And the sea's long grumbling passage.
    These are the words I hear
    Out of the sounds of the sea.
    Alive and suddenly,
    The perfect line breaks clear.
    Trumpet cry in early light! —
    Line of clear carol, medieval, true —
    'There is no Rose of such virtúe'
    Repeating out of winter night —
    'There is no Rose of such virtúe.'

FIFTEENTH CENTURY COMPOSER 1995

Fry's music in the fifteenth century —
What does it matter, now, if nobody knows
Where he lived? — at Chertsey or Ely, he had
The joy of creating beautiful passages
And motets, and no one can invade him
With grubby speculation. There's no respect
In modern times, for closer knowledge. It
Is better to be known only by your
Contribution, not in the spreading stains
Of modern journals — dirty authorship.
Let them keep their levels and he his.
We live in an age of gutter denominators,
At the canine level. His music is played
Around the world, and on his level, enjoyed.

15th Century — Walter Fry. "Alas, Alas, is my chief song".
Lived at Bruges? — One of very many wonderful pieces.

QUEEN CASSIOPEA AND ANDROMEDA

Lullaby, lullaby —
The onomatopoeia
For bringing on of sleep.
Sweet lullabies she wove —
Magical Cassiopea —
Gently round her lovely daughter
Until the nestling turned to graceful dove.
To keep her safe amongst fierce feelings deep
She sang her into loving, true and warm,
Angering the barbarous god of water
Whose nereids longed also for a true love.
Fearing she would drive out their savage charm,
Poseidon chained the girl to the wild sea,
Till Perseus came and set his true love free.

KING OF THE TREES
A Very Haughty Squirrel

He looked at me, straight into my eyes, proudly,
Through the kitchen window, from his place
On a fence post, with huge eyes of power
And strength — close — his whole body muscular
And glossy. He had been examining
(Upside down) the contents of the bird feeder,
And drinking at the pool. With a deft arm
He had pulled up the plastic, guarding nuts
From starlings, to see if he could feed there,
But found wire netting in the way of his teeth.
He stared at me, seated above me, a long time —
Eye to eye, as I stood smiling at him.
He saw nothing funny, only a fool
In a kitchen, grinning through the glass...

MAGIC GROUND AND SLEEPING BEAUTY, WILTSHIRE

Somebody, still, cleverly farms this land;
Some family, invisible to the eye
Of passers-by — wizards of husbandry
In their own acreage — but the old house — why? —
Worn, stranded monster, invented by ghostly life
And then abandoned to the ghosts of it.
Why this seemingly empty, great piece of beauty?
Strange, grey, turreted spread of an old manor,
Lumbering, slumbering, holding itself together
In its sleep. It *looks* as if it snores. I've heard it!
Kingston House, at Kingston Deverill.
And, crazily, here, the Wylye and the Stour,
Snake off through nearby meadows, north and south
Round different counties, and still meet in the sea!

NEWBORN BEAUTY

Girl in light dress, circumscribing lively zones —
Figure and voice in provocative good style,
Shimmering, graceful, with a most disgraceful
Innocent — irresistible boy's tones,
Used with damaging femininity.
Her provocation is a classroom guile,
Educated in suspect clarity —
From Finishing School, with deadly finish in it.
Her newborn eyes, lashed, make their *coups-de-grâce.*
She offers hope of lovely compromise —
Like fragrant surrender to a kiss while dancing.
And all's sweet show — all ping-pong play with glancing,
All time's to spend, with admiration, joke.
She offers pale shoulders to cover with her cloak.

ANGSANA PLACE, SINGAPORE

Angsana Place! I have named it for the trees —
Slender, high-spreading, in their golden blossom,
Across the front of this fine old mansion,
A big house reconstructed into beauty.
The small owner called me away — 'Phil! Phil!
Come and name our house, before it is finished.'
And so I walked round till I saw the Angsanas,
Fountains of light, at the front of the rebuilt house.
All round, the place is green — green Singapore —
Dark waving arboretum, to the botanic
Gardens, cool waves of shade, the houses share,
Built into tropical cover and forested hill.
I won a skip for the name — a delight of laughter
From my wife's small friend, and she clapped her hands at it.

THE NOBLES OF TOSCANA

Low pitched, yet pointed roofs, wide, on three stories,
Tall windows, low arched, in a pale of old rusty farmhouse,
Terracotta, red tiled, spreading its wings.
Below are vineyards and the olive orchards,
In a broad Tuscan acreage — green skirts.
It is flanked by more buildings with olive presses of stone
And the grape vats, walled yards and cypress trees,
Here's Tuscany in every shade of green.
Here's gold and blue — dark green, dark gold, dark blue,
And every shade of brown, grey brown and russet,
Sepia and umber, copper, and old bronze,
And the unforgettable burnt sienna.
Deep blue shines over silver olive green,
And cerulean lapis lazuli,
Over dark spokes of umbrella pines and black
And blue and purple bruising of the grapes.
Under the great sovereign of hot brilliance
Are gentle slopes, all dressed in parallels —
Tarabarella in the Tuscan hills!
The golden broom, now, is ablaze in it,
Setting the hills on fire, burning the hedges.
Tarabarella with cars and carts and tractors
And workers everywhere, or silent, abandoned —
Tarabarella in lovely, lonely beauty.
Century after century you've grown
Out of West Italy, earth of Etruscan
Nobles, who came out of the setting sun
With sails — from where nobody now can tell.
Sails? — who knows where the god first filled their curves,
Made pregnant by his blue Aeolian wind,
That raised the hackles on eternal turquoise
And pressed men on beyond all known survival.
They spread in after many days, a skein
Of wild swans, driving in, with star-led guidance,
The follow-my-leaders, with encouraging cries
And passionate instinct, over unknown waters
Washing Livorno, and beached in a green bay,
Settling inland, with all horizons spent.
Was it an early Columbus, who came searching
The other way, and found this fertile land

More promising than arid Southern Spain?
Perhaps they came from Tyre and were the first
Of all those dark, danger-men, who later sailed
Out of the Pillars — wood shells on a wild Ocean —
To find out Britain, with their well-corded bales.
Perhaps they came in the time of great King Hiram
When King Solomon reigned and was in close alliance
With that Sidonian monarch of Syria.
Or perhaps they sailed from Anatolia —
Weather God-driven Hittite Argonauts,
Sent, running with storms round Western Italy,
Never returning to tell their King, Mursilis;
Or else 'the sailors of Argo', Homer speaks of,
Some of those fifty oarsmen, who met fine women —
(Those pullers on the long oars, in Jason's galley)
And went absent-without-leave, on the way home,
To Iolchis, and fathered a great tribe
Of Grecian heroes, here, in Tuscany,
Gladly deserting the Fleece, for this calm splendour —
The first men ever to settle in Tarabarella.

THE MYSTERY SHIP

When war began in nineteen thirty nine
We had, in the Navy, several "Mystery ships".
They were captained by unusual officers,
And were inherited from the previous war.
They had a roving commission west of Britain
In the approaches and the Irish Sea;
Intended to catch unwary submarines
On the surface and other nefarious vessels,
And to patrol in secrecy, about their work.
They had a strange silhouette, with midship funnel
Like small, low, merchant ships and painted black.
They had quite a good turn of speed, however.
On a dark night (if you could see one, then)
It looked like nothing on earth — sort of hell-on-sea.
They had letters and numbers and no names.
We used to think they were meant to look like trawlers,

But they were too big for that, as we discovered,
Whilst hunting the enemy with our equipment.
One black night, we caught *P.C.74!* —
Skulking round Rathlin Island — off the north
East Coast of Ulster, and didn't know what to make
Of her, except to sink her, and readied our guns
As we crept round, close, to have a better look,
Going to "Action Stations" and closing up.
Then we challenged — it was lucky that we did!
Nobody had seen anything like her before.
We thought she was German, but she replied
In code, satisfactorily, and smartly,
And identified as *P.C.74*.
It was just as well we didn't get nasty.
She could have dropped her dummy bulwarks, at once,
And opened fire with her big guns, unmasked —
And a most destructive force. "What are you doing?"
Our Captain asked cautiously, by soft blue light.
"Shh! — being secret" — was the laconic reply;
And we could get no more. We believed their Captain
Was annoyed at being discovered, as we were bound
To log the matter, and report it back to Base.
So we left him alone, in his harsh seas.
That captain, of course, did have a real name,
But I have forgotten it — a Commander,
He was always known as "*P.C.74*".
He had left the R.N. between the wars,
To become a whaling captain in the Arctic,
Eventually, and had rejoined for service
In the Navy, when war was imminent.
He had been chosen for the job. He was
Gigantic, grey bearded. I remember him
Weaving down Falmouth High Street, later on
In the war, after leaving "The Bunch Of Grapes",
His Arctic oilskins flapping in the wind,
Making him twice his usual staggering size,
And tacking about like a duck in a thunderstorm,
Taking all the road of a Falmouth bus.
He once appeared out of a stormy night —
Nobody knew from where — out of the sea —
Seeking to join a Dance in the North of Scotland,
At a Village Hall. They didn't like him at all, there,
And wouldn't sell him a ticket, when he asked

Quite civilly, waiting in half a gale,
To be let in to lighted festivities,
And they stood in front of the blacked-out entrance,
And asked him who he was. When he replied
"*P.C.74*", they slammed the doors
And bolted them against him, and his protests;
And they phoned the police, to say "a mad giant
Spy, was claiming to be a policeman." It took
Half his ship's company to bail him out.

NAKED BARBARIC BEAUTY

Great Wilton House stands under Salisbury Plain —
Home of the Earls of Pembroke for centuries.
But high on the wild Plain, and by decree
Of the Stone Age hierarchic king —
Raised bare and sacred there, to greet a star,
And ruling in ancient and sidereal grandeur,
Built of Pembroke and Sarsen Stone — Stonehenge!
Strange, too, it is, that from the far Welsh coast
Of Pembroke, were lugged the monstrous blue stones of it,
From the Prescelly Mountains to Stonehenge!
It has stood alone for long millennia,
Unrivalled Temple in all of Northern Europe.
It is ruined now, but near five thousand years old.
Stonehenge was begun before the Beaker Culture.
This sun-worshipping temple was first sited
By Stone Age shepherd-priests, with posts and Heel Stone
And wooden building structures, ditch and bank,
To command the rolling, bare, surrounding plain,
A peaceful grazing ground in Northern Europe,
Even before Great Britain was an island!
Then nomad tribes settled here and multiplied,
Under their Beaker Culture's shepherd-king.
On their sea journeys, they had found Milford Haven.
Far-voyaging explorers, in their canoes,
Had gone up-river, foraging, and had seen
Natural quarries of loose bluestone boulders.
They sledged and floated home, their eight ton burdens,
From the Prescelly Mountains in west Wales,
Out of Milford Haven, all the way,

Lashed to large dug-out trimaran canoes —
Coastwise by sea, to the wide Severn River,
Travelling in convoys to guard their monoliths,
Floating and punting them, day after day,
Led by the stars — moon after moon of time,
Through forest land, dark valleys and the plain,
Across the West Country, to this spreading downland —
On the Bristol Avon, Frome and Wylye rivers,
And the Salisbury Avon, northward to Stonehenge.
So, sledging and floating, they came to their Sacred Site,
And round the old building, began their engineering.
They raised this first Temple, to glow under the sun.
They raised these monoliths up, and bedded them deep
With a true science, a propitiating worship —
With awesome, and with accurate proportion.
They ramped, and stood them up, just as the Heel Stone
Had been set up for the sun, so long before.
The axis was established with the Station Stones,
And aligned on sunrise at Midsummer Day.
They circled the stones with faith, for the sun's worship,
With God-fearing, careful, weather-beaten pride;
For the majestic ball was their god then,
And mid-summer Solstice their great Time of Times —
The solstitial moments as the Earth dipped down,
And lit the Heel Stone through to the circle's centre.
Stonehenge was long begun, before this time —
Before the late Neolithic Beaker People —
A kingdom of wide, rolling shepherd pasture,
Green horizons, great herds, and the Avon River;
Where summers blaze and winter storms abound.
Later, in Bronze Age time, tremendous stones —
The fifty ton Sarsen Stones, were sledged across
From quarries less than thirty miles to the north,
By the Vale of Pewsey, and added to the building,
Tooled, dressed, morticed and tenoned overhead!
So this priestly kingdom was crowned with beauty,
And we must keep it free and bare for ever.
It is a green and proud and absolute duty.

THE IDIOTICON

What somebody once said under the sun
On a windy beach ... smell of old seaweed ...
With a brown-streaked ancient tanker coming up
Into the river and never gaining
Much against the turning tide. The salt
Wide-open estuary
Swallowing the ship's efforts — grey sea-serpent —
River of threat, with anger a mile wide
Full of dark navigation buoys, rejected,
Leaning from the tide that turns against them.
Boats buried in the beach, and upside down.
Great gulls strutting about in charge, that shout
Like vixens, and the chocolate melting
          Grittily in our teeth.

CHELTENHAM GOLD CUP *11th November 1995*

Twelve runners with great names, like Bradbury Star,
And Buckboard Bounce, Egypt Mill Prince and Coulton,
For the two and a half mile, famous steeplechase.
They got away for a magical, thrilling gallop,
And covered dead ground full of a gutsy action,
While the racing Cheltenham rain was pelting down.
Brendan Powell was riding Dublin Flyer,
And crowned his career with his handling of the horse.
They jumped as one, together, with muscular rhythm,
Fighting with Egypt Mill Prince, who began to gain.
As Oaksey said, they stared at defeat up the hill,
And stared it out of countenance, and passed it —
Clawing back the lead — the stylish Dublin Flyer —
Stretching last muscular call, on the cruel hill, home.

LAKE DISTURBANCE

Racket of pigeons escaping — thrashing wings
Bursting out through high arched branches
To the west sky, bright, over serious woods.
As I stepped into still, waterside aisles, here,
A desperate liberty was captured, mere
Terrorised seconds — sky-need
Wing-flash and wild break out — panic release,
Clatter and scatter of violent exit
Across polished water — pure escape and gone.
        I was left alone.
Silence spread out, thinly, after bird flight,
And calm was solemnly reinstated,
    Under the canopy that translated
    Sudden freedom into evening light.

HIGH CARNAVAL AND HIGH SOCIETY

When I was young and on my training ship,
HMS *Worcester*, I had a Peruvian friend —
A Cadete Naval, in the Peruvian Navy,
Who was training with me. His family
Lived in Lima, and when my ship reached there,
I paid him a visit. They had a fine house.
High Carnaval ran wild for two weeks. He had
A pretty sister, whom I liked, and she
Liked me. But marriage was all — likings held nothing
For conservative society in old Lima,
With no airports. You couldn't hold a girl's hand.
You could smile and speak praise, but girls were kept
Behind iron bars — so they just smouldered and smiled.
She sent me her photo — but then World War began.

SWANS OVER THE HOUSE

Swans over the house, crossing above our roof,
Say forty feet up, in irregular wedge shape
Formation — mother and cygnets — the soft voice
Of the leader, turning head back to them
Gently, and the soft call — an oboe note
Of guidance. I think they were flying across
From Longleat and heading for the small lake
At Leighton House, not a great journey. They
Seemed under instruction. That was how it looked.
A beautiful tableau in flight — arresting,
It was passing in effortless slow time,
A snowy dream procession, moving over
Our tiles, so low, and delicately, though
Such large birds sailed through air, cumulus-pale,
Calm clouds in a vision, pale necks advanced
Into geometry of a smooth glide.
So they went on down toward lake water —
Elegant yachts, with wind-wise spread of sail.

THE SPANISH CIVIL WAR *(London) (For Maureen Dufferin)*

I remember the Spanish Restaurant
In Swallow Street, with Pepe at the door.
How cheerful he was and sociable — Pepito,
In all he did for the bright Thirties' crowd —
Cars drawing up with diners and those others
With schooners of fine sherry on their minds.
He had the news about the Civil War —
Of how the war was going, week by week.
At times he would say "I've got a holiday
For a few months". (He took long holidays!)
But we all knew he had gone back to fight,
And time would wait for Pepe at the war …
"We'll win!" — but he was wrong — and time ran out
At last, and he never came back any more.

THE FIRST DAWN

The black silhouette of cock-crow and the skies —
The bird of dawning in his dark valley cries
Shouting out, as his world rolls there, revealing
Rim of new day! Egg after broken egg,
And a proud stance — what is there to say?...
His call has never been tuned to us at all.
He has brought his ancient worship of the sun
Out of the egg, through all these millennia.
Sealed in, his fanfare has been breaking out
For thousands of vanished ceremonial years,
Through the echo of the still egg — the silence
That contains it — egg giving birth to egg,
And sound to sound — proud office to greet the light,
Since breaking from the first egg, first made day bright!

WESTERN WIND?

John Taverner began composing music
With courtly songs and in the glittering pageant
And golden settings of King Henry the Eighth.
Perhaps he wrote the greatest of all that glory —
Most memorable and beautiful and wild
Of all the Tudor live-for-ever love songs —
The beseeching —'Westron wynde when will thow blow?'
His Masses are medieval music, in time
Of Renaissance, with Flemish influence —
Just as King Henry the Seventh's Palace was
Built with Burgundian tutelage, and not
Sired by the great Masters in the South. Did John
Fall in love with his Lady In The Tower
Of Music? When was his 'Western Wind Mass' born?

John Taverner, Boston, Lincolnshire 1490–1545

A NOISY NIGHT'S HISTORY

The storm reared snarling, with frozen talons
Of snow, over the wild escarpment
Above us here, at Westbury and tore
At our tiles, before the night was ended.
Day showed its claw marks, white
Down the bare side of Salisbury Plain,
Where we shelter. The Duke of York
Murdered our bishop, just overhead, here;
And The Ridgway links Lyme Regis to The Wash
In Lincolnshire — full of tramping Roman
Soldiers — all the way to Boston Stump,
Where Taverner lies, whose Masses rang through Europe,
Concealed from Cromwell's iconoclastic thugs —
Great music, murder, civil wars and storm.

CARTWHEELS

Eating roast chestnuts and drinking wine
With little sauced mounds of *écrevisses bordelaises*,
Amongst cork trees, somewhere south in the Auvergne,
We sniffed the roasting scents of early Autumn
On a wooded, clouded, mountain side,
As we listened to far sounds.
After local laughter above the river,
And — "pourquoi?"..."mais non!"..."parce que"..."à ma connaissance" —
The wings of a spiralling bird
For the eyes' silence.
And for the heart of it, there were great wheels,
Iron-shod, below us, echoing in a vineyard,
"à là!... allez!" — staggering hooves, loaded
Wagon wheels — straining harness — great horses goaded.

DARK AGE OF UNQUIET SEA

I sometimes wake to hear it in the night
Distantly, the sound of winter sea.
Far out it has a different kind of sound,
It is a lament, yet never quite the same —
Unequal, solemn reproach, in the wild cold,
A constant motion, constantly unquiet,
Some great injustice, muttering out of mind.
Nearer to me there is a kind of chorus,
Slow dance of waves, mourning on the sea shore —
Question, answer, often repeated there,
Without a satisfaction, half a comfort,
The answer becomes what the question was, before —
"Let us be patient, charitable and kind",
Often repeated with monotonous care.

CRACKED CITY — FIN DE SIÈCLE

The spirit rising from this place is ancient,
The beauty is still young in its old youth.
It is a place lost in dark passages
Of time, great art, and noble ceremony,
Long violence, false witness, stealthy poison.
The tree-lined gracious boulevards to the river,
Are flanked by pillared arcades and floral parks,
And palaces of proud Imperial past.
But its behaviour and its beliefs have altered,
It is a place lost in its own translation.
The city has emerged with spilled-out treasure
Wasted on trash, exploiting loud group noises,
Failed arts, and show business greed, depraved by drugs.
Computers broadcast envy and bestial crime.

PANAMA

I shall always remember the colours blazing,
The tropical shine of the entrance to the Canal
At Panama — outlandish, exciting, spicy,
Even the naughty nightclubs they had there —
Cuban cigar smoke, scented lovelies, darkness
And wine, the turbulent music's incessant beat,
Celebrating erotic and outrageous night-shows,
Sixty years ago. It was smart to sail
Across the blue Gulf of Mexico to the tropics,
From a free Cuba, on a great British liner,
White, awning-covered, lazy, to Colon —
The beautiful Reina Del Pacifico —
Out of that old pirate harbour, Havana.
One wore the minimum of flimsy clothing
As the ship moved on and through to the Pacific,
Linked to electric towing-mules, like tanks
That approached along the hot concrete to hook up
And pull you through the locks, on either side
Of the huge ship, in short black shadow and dazzle
Of Central America — brilliant paint and awnings,
Attended by the squat little trams on rails,
With enormous and efficient pulling power.
The American military were in the Canal
Zone, in their pale uniforms, lazily smart,
They had low, red-roofed barracks, under shade trees.
There were sudden crashing purple, thunderstorms,
Like no other in ferocity of sound —
The flash and battery of almost incessant lightning,
Sheet and zigzag, smell of gunpowder, thunder —
Fire, brimstone, bellowing, unbelievable —
Deafening violence — shuddering to the ears.
You were soaked at once, if you stayed out.
Then everything fell quiet in blazing heat,
And thin white uniform dried on you at once.
The electric towing-mules cast off their cables,
And the ship was free to continue through the Canal
Lakes — on through the Isthmus of Darien —
Old Darien of the Conquistadors,
Of Cortez, and his first sight of the Pacific!
The Royal Road from Nombre de Dios Bay,
He staggered through, can now be passed by water!

In the narrows, monkeys climbed above you,
And alligators, near twenty feet long, slid down
Into lake water. All was spicily wild,
Green, brilliant and alive. Birds called and blazed
In colour. The forest screamed aloud for miles —
From above, to miles away inland. The pilot
High on the bridge, with cigar, was American,
Drawling Southern wisecracks to the ship's captain.
We were in the American Canal Zone,
From which, I think, the Americans have withdrawn, now.
I met the old actor, Edward Arnold, there,
In the port of Colon, one day, near dawn,
In a nightclub, at his table, enjoying a show —
More like a film than on any of his locations.
The villages were full of lively people.
There were brilliant red roofs and equally vivid
Green clearings, amongst luxuriant growth
Of fruiting palms. Our tropical white was blinding,
The military and Central American beauty
Contrasted; yet all seemed elegant and rich,
In those peaceful days of nineteen thirty five.
Every scene was startlingly bright coloured —
In flashy colour, yet soft, and like no other
I've seen, anywhere, in this colourful world.
And Panama City! "See Panama City" they said,
"And dance, desnudo, all the way back in your
Panama Hat!" But I never saw the intrepid
Returning, to know if they were taken like that.

YOU HAVE TO BE HUNGRY IN HEAVEN

Valdivia in South Chile, that fine Welsh harbour!
I remember it, Patagonian-bright, when young.
I went ashore there, early, expecting nothing
But sheep, and found a noble brewery —
A German exile's functional dreaming tower,
Looking over the houses to Welsh sheep pastures.
But the breakfast they made for me beside that temple!
Was paradisal English bacon and eggs — bright
Like the morning sun! — Locally smoked, new laid,
And fried in Welsh churned butter, with fresh bread.
No breakfast could compare — the beer was rare! —
Served in the far South, by a pretty Welsh girl.
It is all I imagine an exile's heaven to be —
Brew-cultured, coffee-fragrant, with a girl singing.

Valdivia, South America 1936 (S. Chile in Patagonia)
Bach's Cantata No. 8 and "Canta y no llores!"

THE WELSH BORDER

Goodrich Castle is the precipice of all
Medieval strength destroyed, and yet
Not destroyed at all — great towered escarpment,
Terrifying, brutal, or, as you will,
A peace-preserving terror in massive stone.
Armed to the arrow slits above the valley —
Old blood-red stones, the size of motor cars,
If history is solid dream — this is it.
It is a volcanic eruption over the valley
That threatens to erupt again, out of broken tubes.
Its violence continues massively still.
It holds the border with full rending beast claws,
And never will let go, nor cease to send
Out horrifying threat, to the world's end.

BUM-BOAT JOSÉ *Cape Verde Islands 1936*

Bum-boat José, rowing out at midnight,
Lounging in the stern-sheets, with his sons at the oars,
And the warm night airs bringing spice from the island
And far wild rhythms from the starlit shores.

Riding out at anchor, off the Cape Verde Islands,
Unloading cargo — time wasting in the sun;
We longed to land there, we didn't have authority —
Exotic the marvels and the treasure to be won.

Strange birds flew to us, and settled in the rigging,
Surging, longing, we rode green island seas.
Cape Verde, magical, we heard them calling us —
Warm island voices — temptations of the breeze.

Bum-boat José, rowing out at midnight,
Selling mystery and gemstones, fine gold, pearls,
Cigars out of Cuba, flower scent, Bacardi,
Island love and promises, and songs from the girls.

FURTHER FLIGHT, THE JOCKEY CLUB CUP *Newmarket 1995*

Further Flight, the old racehorse, put down his head,
And began his run late, from the back of the field,
With Michael Hills, great son of a great Trainer —
Barry Hills. Now, Further Flight is like one
Of their family — four times running, the winner
Of The Jockey Club Cup, and looking for his fifth!
The grey began his late run from the rear,
Head down, ears back, and going like the wind.
He saw daylight, and nothing could stop him then —
The other good horses spent, and going back,
As if worn out — they had opened up too soon,
Perhaps. But grabbing the ground, the true old athlete,
Just went for his further flight and passed them by,
From the back to the front and the post for the fifth time running!

AUTUMN THING

When leaves curl, slimy underfoot
And cling to panes, and toadstools thrive
In greasy clumps, and birds are wet,
And singing's done in trees, and some blow down,
And flowers are gone, and everyone
To keep alive,
Looks for a jab against the 'flu,
Whatever shall we do?
We'll drive away through tunnelled rain,
Past muddy dig-up, trench and cone,
To the wet airport and complain —
We'll have a moan.
And we'll buy tickets to the gold
Las Palmas sun, and stay until we're old.

THE MERLINS OF FORSINARD

Specially for H.M. Queen Elizabeth, The Queen Mother (who likes it).
(Background music "Sanctus Arcticus" also Taverner's "Mass of the Western Wind")

The Merlins of Forsinard — I have read about them
Again — in the Flow Country, around Caithness.
I was in Thurso, its little capital once.
I could look across towards the lochans, southwards
Out over lands of the Black Throated Diver,
Lands of the Greenshank and the Golden Plover,
The Widgeon, the Arctic Skua wheeling high.
They are treeless, unprotected bare horizons
In bitter weather, wind shouting at my windows,
        Clawing at the glass. Voices —
Wild voices fill The Mass Of the Western Wind.
Then the sun shafts out across the town
From the Halladale River, from the shining Flowland,
The last wet wilderness — at the Pentland Firth!
Bright steel-wild water network, lochans, moorland,
Sphagnum and heather, tussock and peat bog; sunny
Wind horizons — the wide world round — surround.
They are empty, except for a multitude of birds.

In fact, birds are busy right to Cape Wrath —
All across, beseeching, hunting, forlorn,
And crying out in the crying out of the wind.
Past wind-eroded crofts and villages,
They are feeding, mating, tumbling about in the sky.
It is a great, wild, rare population,
        Massed celebration.
Carved, silent, trigger-fast Merlins watch there,
In the freshest air left in the Western World!
And I remember it still, I think of it now.
That day I collected my Orkney beagle,
I had rescued over in Kirkwall,
To give him good retirement in Devon,
When the Argyll and Sutherland Hunt broke up.
I said goodbye to Northern Patrol,
And to those storm-dangerous thundering seas,
And to my ship, *Northern Princess*.
Then I said goodbye to Thurso and the Flow,
And the Palace there; and the Castle by Loch Mey,
And the silent Merlins of Forsinard — the Falcons.
Beagle and I were going home...
The Bailie beareth the bell away.

Afterwards HMS *Northern Princess* was sunk with all hands, off Iceland, and all my crew lost. I was glad to have served the last Emperor. Now it is all finished. The Q.M. likes this poem.

SURPRISE ON A VOYAGE TO ABERDEEN

One ship I served in was *Northern Princess*,
During the last war — on Northern Patrol —
Off Iceland, which the allies occupied.
We watched, far out, in fearful seas for German
Battleships breaking out to the Atlantic,
Patrolling on our beam-ends until relieved
For a brief week on shore and some repairs.
We had "heavy seas down the funnel" trouble,
And a cottage meal back on firm ground was fine.
Our admiral was based at Reykjavic.

We were ordered to bring him home on leave
With his Staff. I was second-in-command,
And arranged a special surprise for him,
On the way home. One of our officers
Volunteered to produce a first class dinner —
It was Lieut. the Hon. Lyulph Stanley,
(Who had a West End flat, with chef to match.)
He was amusing — an agreeable fellow,
And so I let him take over in the galley,
Making him chef for the night to show his skill,
On the thousand mile voyage to Aberdeen.
We were rather bored with all the good fresh fish
We caught in those seas, as was the Admiral;
So Lyulph began with soup — a Russian Bortsch —
Leading to Slavic joys which I forget now.
It was a very well-planned meal and also,
In those cold, rolling seas, very well cooked.
The *chef d'oeuvre* at the end, was to be truly
A masterpiece — an enormous rum omelette,
Floating in spirit and lit at the last moment,
For a dramatic entrance from sea-darkness.
We had planned it all. Lieutenant Stanley
Would have to burst in with a great frying pan
From the galley — along the heaving deck —
With the Sou' Wester blowing, and then light up
In the wardroom, bearing Rum Omelette Surprise!
I was helping him, and had deputed
Myself to be Master of Ceremonies.
So I left the table, and conversation
Of our Captain, and his agreeably fed
Officers, dining with the Admiral,
And his staff. They were more than expectant.
But Lyulph had never set fire to naval rum
Before, and had been very liberal with it.
I stood by the ward-room door, and as soon as
I heard the heavy steps of his arrival,
I flourished it open, to admit this monster,
Who blew in, lighting the vast pan, and bearded
Like the pard, but he tripped over the coaming
Passing me — spread eagled with a roar
Of flames — and the whole explosive mixture
In his frying pan, was discharged across the room
At the diners, and burst against the table —

A sort of disintegrating Halley's Comet —
Setting fire to the carpet and the Base Accountant,
Who climbed on his chair, beating himself out.
The Admiral remarked amongst the flames
That this was "much worse than the war" — in his
Opinion. The dinner party dispersed
For fire-fighting activities, round the table,
And beating out the carpet and the Commander
(Accounts) who was still a bit on fire.
The Admiral was cheerful about it all —
The omelette had been a monumental surprise! —
It seemed he had seldom known such a flambéed
Dinner Party, and the story would remain
One of the best of his war recollections.
We were not so sure about the Commander,
He had suffered the broadside of a flying omelette.

AFTER ALAMEIN

I

I remember sitting in that hot gold desert
Beside the Canal with Arabs, or with Colonel
Beresford, overshadowed by ships, their propellers
Thundering the water beside us, coming through
From Suez to Port Said — or sitting on a camel
With a rifle strapped to the back of the saddle,
In Naval white uniform, with my army
Friends in khaki, at the end of the trail,
From Sinai to the Egyptian camel market.
The Arabs kept stealing bits of the railway line
Because they needed the metal, I believe,
To make their guns. Beresford was a gunner
Resting from Alamein. I have often wondered
What happened to that brave man, after we won.

II

Beresford's family were in the timber business.
He went over to Poland before the war,
Buying standing timber out of their forests,
For shipment back to England. He used to tell me
How beautiful Poland was before invasion —
And, no doubt, still is — the great wide plains and hills.
We floated rough-made toy boats in the Canal,
And then threw stones at them, and I taught him
Close-range spotting, gunnery rules, we used
At sea. It was absorbing, as we talked
Together, resting on the hot bank of the Suez
Canal, with Arabs watching and talking too.
We discussed a book called "And Mr Wyke Bond".
We liked Mr Bond, we agreed — he helped old ladies.

My ship had been HMS *Antwerp* — Anti-Aircraft Cruiser. We had been working on the flank of the 8th Army. I had been temporarily in command, and had been recommended for command of a Destroyer.

BUTTER STREET IN ALCESTER

Butter Street in Alcester runs around
Behind the fine church of St. Nicholas,
With its square tower of a pale lichen grey —
Or, in the sunlight, an ancient greenish gold,
And everything surrounding the church is splendid.
Front, back and sides no-one has ever knocked
Anything down — just kept it fairly upright.
The whole High Street, with Butter Street forming
A necklace for the church, is a heavenly Tudor
Survival harbour, apart from the Georgian Church House,
The Verger's House — Georgian beautiful too,
And the house of the Veterinary Surgeon.
Nothing much has really fallen down
All the way down the High Street. The town is live,
And everything has simply gone on working

Without the quilted smocks and doublet and hose.
All the way out to Mary Arden's house,
Through Shakespeare's green cocoon of evolution —
From Walcote to Wilmcote, it is a marvel
Of suckling colour and bright age. The fields are
Shakespeare green, June green. Arcadian
Alcester sings like a blackbird in its trees,
Beyond main traffic and roads, it sings all summer.
People drive to Stratford-upon-Avon
And leave this town alone, with its own honey
And knowledgeable bees of history,
Amongst those banks where the wild thyme still grows.
They lead a quiet, midland working life here,
With a small independent economy,
With D.I.Y. and Hardware shops and cafés;
But the Tudor farms have Arden dairies still,
And their own honie-suckle of content.

GO FROM MY WINDOW

Love's ancient mariners just run aground,
As I've done — long ago, between spring tides —
Taken the beach, in a reach of the wide river,
Stuck fast beside deep woodland, high and dry,
Like an old house, listing. 'Go from my window'
Sang Orlando Gibbons. Go from my window
Too, Love, leave me alone. I am too old
For teasing and lingering eyes. Stir your young men.
Race them, uncaught, get them to gasp for you,
You can easily keep the winner if you need him,
But your appetite is all for thrills and spills.
Me? — I have gone aground — but not for love!
Thought has caught up with me, and you can never
Float me off ... Oh! — go from my window, love.

Orlando Gibbons 1583–1625 Composer (on the Viol)

ABSOLUTE — WHAT IS REVEALED — IS

Driving along the road to Shepton Mallet
As I often do, the sun broke through,
While I was glancing south, down flowing country
And all the sloping park land came alight.
And I saw the turrets and spires in a green fire.
It was All-Hallows in sublimated time —
Heart-melting chivalry of the old days,
Far more beautiful than when near-by —
Than the solid thing — a sumptuous promise,
A beckoning to cloistered paradise.
There is the part of things at certain times
And distances, unsolid, the form distilled.
And there is, in such material, a promise
Revealed, and through dark shadow of glass, fulfilled.

Cranmore Hall, Somerset 1995

GUN HILL, BARBADOS

Climb up this green, commanding eminence
Of Gun Hill, in Barbados, and look down
Across the sea, beyond the bay at Consett,
Where Cromwell's ships stood in, with cannonade.
The wind blows over the map beneath you
And slings rain into your face. Here the invasion
Became a rout. Up here, Lord Willoughby,
With well-armed troops stood firm and tumbled Cromwell.
After the King's murder, he changed allegiance,
And sickened by radical, religious hatreds,
Joined us out here, to fight the King's enemies.
They never got up this hill and we outflanked them.
They made an accommodation at the foot.
Caught between us, they withdrew at sea level.

Lord Willoughby of Parham.

MR THOMAS MAYCOCK'S PAVAN.

The old judge who lived above the bay
Used to say, looking down towards the headland,
"There's old Mr Maycock gazing out to sea —
I fancy he moves his head." It is a great grey
Coral rock massif, in the shape of a man
Standing up — a man in a peruke,
Steadfast and strong. Ronald Taylor knew
The old judge well, long before he met me —
A man well-travelled in the Caribbean —
A scholar, with many strange tales of the sea
And the Islands, but more about Barbados,
Back to the time when it was empty forest.
I should like to have met him, before he died.
I would like to have stood up here and gazed
Out with him at grey old Mr Maycock.
I would have liked to tell him we saw the old fellow
Making a slow measured dance of it,
On the coral shore, to the sound of the sea —
As it was performed there, some have said, when
We first found it — uninhabited —
But he would have been dancing a galliard then.

Maycock Town, Barbados 1993

BARBADOS — TALKATIVE VICAR GETS TRANSLATED...ETC

Alongside Maycocks Bay lies Rupert Bay.
After Prince Rupert's unbeaten cavalry
Could no longer bring victory to the King, his uncle,
Against successful Cromwell, he led the loyal
Part of his Navy in the Caribbean,
With the same invincible prowess, in sea-fights
Against the Commonwealth convoys, which he harried,
Based on Dominica and Barbados.
There's a legend he was married in our church.

Years later, a Hanoverian frigate arrived,
And removed the vicar of St Lucy,
With all the church records, and some parishioners.
Sugar's sweet, rum talks — but who was "bonny"...?
With vicars of Bray or St Lucy — who was safe then?

Maycocks Bay, St Lucy, Barbados. W.I

There's a rumour they fell overboard in a storm — even that the vicar got made a bishop. The islanders seem to have been stunned or overawed. One thing is quite certain — they got the wrong man.

HAROLD BOWEN, THE BARBADOS AUCTIONEER

"What am I bid for this glass vase, my friends?"
Asked Harold. "It has a crack in its bottom" —
Turning it sadly upside down — "a fault,
Alas, from which we all suffer." He sighed
At it, inclining his head — a clergyman
At his congregation — such words would bring
On the eruption of an immense black lady
In one of the wide window seats. Her friends
Would hold on to her as she was heaving
And wheezing uncontrollably — the outburst
When it came deafened everyone, and Harold
Would wait until the volcano had died down.
These smaller sales were mostly for household lots,
It was a weekly treat, here, just to attend.
"Do not engage mouth, till brain has been started!"
Was a friendly caution to the over hasty,
Excitedly bidding against themselves,
Or for the wrong lot, in the midst of gossip.
"I dare not ask your hand, dear lady — indeed
I do not seek so high", he would quote — and this
About a voluptuous Victorian nude
With collapsing drapery — a print, his porter
Was holding up. His auction room was always
Filled with loud country laughter from the cane
Sugar circles, teachers, local housewives,

And a mixed following of Bajan people —
Kind, with mild gossip, noisy until quelled
With magisterial voice, to get at brisk bidding.
"Ladies! ladies!" the auctioneer would cry —
"Kindly go home to exchange your local news!"
When he couldn't compete against the glorious hubbub.
He also handled the far grander auctions
In the great houses, full of valuables,
With a more dignified ceremony of course.
Harold Bowen could be most impressive,
But still his saucy explosives set the crowd laughing.
He was comfortably round, Welsh stock and jovial,
He had powerful understanding of our people.
Dealers came from many of the Islands
In the Caribbean — even from England
And America, for the important sales.
His knowledge of fine antiques had been gained well,
Particularly in his favourite subjects,
Of silver and mahogany furniture;
And every sort of local artefact;
And his large, friendly family all helped him,
With Monica, his wife, ruling the finance.
He was seen as an artist in his performances.
His best loved porter was a wiry woman —
An elderly lady, wearing a brown hat,
Aged "seventy five" — as all black ladies are, there,
An age they proudly confess to — never more.
She was as fit as any of his porters,
She was called "E.P.". Harold often hugged her
Before a sale — a lucky warmth of ritual —
And so, sometimes, did I. She was that sort —
Invaluable, unperturbed, dedicated,
She never tired, and knew where everything was.
Harold was very well-known and loved by many
In Barbados and in the other Islands.
In Great House Sales he would start in the kitchen,
Full of copper and brass and crusty woodwork,
With a worm-eaten cupboard — say. A voice calls
"Hey! What dem holes is?" — "Ladies and gents
I'll not fool you — this cupboard got in friends!" —
The delighted fun-lovers fully satisfied.
The scene is a great old Plantation House
Approached up a long driveway with tall, stately

Royal palms making long avenue
And cars parked everywhere round coral sweeps,
Beside green lawns and many flowered trees
Under bold Bajan sun of scented heat —
A mass of cars as far as the old stables
And carriage house. There are a number of planters
Standing, greeting, or chatting, or inside, viewing
The chief items, ranged in the main rooms,
And coming in and out for outside lots.
Inside is a cross section of Barbadians —
Parish folk, townspeople, from round the Island
And a good section of fun-lovers, too,
In for an early morning look and sport.
But we still have the crush in the huge kitchen
And from it invites the Voice — "What am I bid
For this stove? Don't mind if it looks old.
It's like me, to work properly we got to
Warm up first" — This is what he is doing
Lost in the crush, debouching from the last lot
In the kitchen. Then from the kitchen the scene
Moves up to a bedroom next — but not before
The saucy voice has announced an invitation
"Ladies! I'm going in the bedroom". There are many
But they all head for a smaller one, already
Part-filled with would-be bidders, on the beds.
"Where's E.P.?" Harold shouts, and looks about,
Or he calls for one of the other porters there,
His son appears with his clip-board papers,
And Monica with the big book of lots;
And they all get in, somehow, with a camp table,
And a whole lot of the crowd gets in as well.
Harold extols the virtues of bedside lamps —
"They throw a lot of light on the subject."
He always speaks with the warm Bajan accent —
Long ē like "thee" for the definite article.
"Is you sell dem mattress wi' dem beds?"
A bidder asks, meaning are beds being sold
With mattresses and he is told they are — .
But if he doesn't want them, he can put them
"On thee floor and work out Miss Flora " — who?
Is she? — Nobody knows except the bidder,
Drowned by encouraging cries to have a go!
Harold then indicates some bedroom rugs

With memories of a young couple who kept
One in the boot of their car, "to change flat tyres".
But one night, after a flat tyre, they were shocked to find
The car had been stolen. Finally a huge wardrobe
Is said to be so spacious and inviting
That it reminds the speaker of a planter
Friend of his, who told him that his wife
Valued her dresses so highly, that she put
A watchman there, to guard them. It was a fact
His friend had said — one day he'd come home early
And found the watchman right *inside* the thing.
As Harold leaves, after this final item —
"A bargain there, as you can all see, ladies...
It can hold a watchman, or two, for you."
I used to attend all his big auctions
In the main rooms, where the dealers would collect.
Sometimes I bid for lots I could afford
And I did a bit of voluntary work,
Bidding for the Museum, when I was asked,
Or on behalf of owners of big houses
In Barbados, with my wife helping me.
Stephen might want some things for Nicholas[1] —
Pictures, porcelain, furniture and Persian
Carpets, old glass, snuff boxes and the rest.
One of my chief competitors in this work
Was the Ambassador from one of the States
Of South America, whose diplomatic
Bag devoured oil paintings and chandeliers,
Once, even, an almost new Mercedes car.
His agent was well-known to me as well —
(His vain attempt at anonymity!)
Sometimes they would both attend the sale
Supporting each other against the dealers,
And when he stopped bidding, she took over.
(My wife and I did the same, with our own bidding)
Sometimes the agent would ask me my opinion
Knowing of my connection with the Museum,
And that I went to friends' houses to value.
She would ask my opinion before she bid,
And sometimes afterwards, particularly
If I had been trying to buy for the Museum,
And had lost the lot to her, or one of her helpers!
The whole thing was a fairly friendly contest,

Like complex tennis, without the running about.
There were quite a few millionaires at work, there.
(One old lady headed her firm of bankers.)
We had to be in full play, and poker-watchful!
The Museum, under-funded, lost many chances —
For the Island — irreplaceably lost.
Harold lived at beautiful Ebor House,
With his family, not far from the sea,
Where we dined and later went out of doors
Under the Ebony grove in his gardens —
In the green shadow of shadow-fragrancies,
Beside the sea — tropical and magic,
The gossiping Caribbean talking itself drowsy,
Where white peacocks perched in the Ebony. He died
In Florida, soon after he retired.
His going has taken from life in the Caribbean.
And for us all in Barbados, part of its cheer
Has gone. He was a good man, a good friend.

[1] Nicholas Abbey (17th century)

VANCOUVER SIDE 1995

I like the names of towns in the Rocky Mountains
In Canada — Cache Creek, Kamloops and Whistler,
Kicking Horse Pass and Lillooet and Squamish
And far beyond these valleys to Medicine Hat.
The Indian names contain a self-description.
Kamloops is a "coming-together-of-the-waters",
At this expanding, busy river junction,
Still unspoiled. Sicamous — "Squeezed-in-the-middle"
Is between two lakes, and there is Monashee —
Gaelic for peace. All the rivers this side
Of the high forest snows, like the Fraser,
Wash down to the Pacific, about Vancouver.
Beyond the vast ridge, they flow to the Atlantic,
I'll come and live here, in timbered Coquitlam.

ROCKY MOUNTAIN THAW 1995

The black bears wake. Moose feed high up in clearings
And mountain goats tread desperate verticals.
Beaver and deer appear much lower down.
Above them all a megatonnage of ice
And snow. Waters beginning immensely high
Leak through the echoing distances — and near,
Near at hand, interwoven prophecies,
Half sound — hushed silence of dark forest. Falls —
Collapse of a snow-load from a branch of silence
In the raw...
Thaw.
Black bear appears at the forest entrance,
With a half running, half swaying, progress, stopped.
Great bulk, ears, nose, alert — athletic engine
Of aggression, frozen, powerfully ready,
Hungry after hibernation — searching.
It vanishes. Silence then. Snow collapsing.
A stag sneezes — consternation there,
And scamper. Hushed growth of a new silence,
In the raw...
Thaw.
A mega weight hangs towering above.
Rock solid moves on waters in a trough.
With hold lost, all — trees, forest — all must fall.
The father and mother of avalanche will sweep
All in its path. Mountain gone critical.
Soon...après moi...la catastrophe.

CANADIAN TUMBLE-WEED 1995

Sage Brush turns the wide plains bluish green —
Pale carved weeds, inches apart to the horizon,
Massed, shapely miniatures. The late sun spreads
There, sharpening each tight sculpture in relief —
Each an art-form, curvaceously different,
Armies of individual leafy bushes.
Then their golden flowers cover the landscape
And are soon gone, with the bees, greedy for Sage
Nectar. The bushes then run to seed and die
And wind-uprooted, are blown along, tumbling
Under the sun and the starlight, Now they foam
In a coastless sea of somersaulting, pale
Skeletons, a death dance for an eagle's flight.
Honey and seed made, so they tumble away.

JASPER AND BANFF, CANADA 1995

I enjoyed my time at Jasper in Alberta,
A little town growing up by the green forests
Amongst white Rockies — the grey and white of them
And the blue sky. It is modern, crystal clear,
In the fresh oxygen of Canada,
With a friendly people, high on the high border,
From British Columbia, and on the road
To Banff, which I like too, because it has
A mountain at each end of the main street.
They look at each other with their great snow
White faces, surprised at what is sitting there,
Between them, in their laps, with a Hudson Bay
Trading branch, too. Both towns are ski resorts,
Nowhere near much, except Calgary and the sky.

JASPER AND JADE 1995

Jasper and jade from Canada — big pebbles —
Dark holly green of jade, and holly berry
Red of jasper, sealing wax red, and polished,
Softly beautiful, meltingly tactile.
Calming to the heart of the holder of it —
Jade is darkly noble, and veined with peace.
You can buy them in British Columbia,
Heaped in the shops, straight from up-country mines
They gleam in hoards for you to seek with fingers
Buried in their cool glow. Striped amethysts,
Chevron amethysts, are there, bright coloured agates.
Canada is young, a massive beauty,
Overflowing with forests, mountains, lakes,
And friendly people, endlessly interesting.

CANADIAN ROCKIES 1995

For hundreds of miles these cold enormous mountains
Clothed in snow, over cragged rock, stare down.
Along great valleys of bleak sky-blocking peaks,
Their serried, saw-edged shoulders, carry dark forests,
Pine forest cloaks them. Road rides up and down,
And on and on through all the endless valley —
Peaks white against frozen blue, blue-grey with streamers
In every prehistoric monstrous shape.
There are submarines with savage conning towers,
And fleets of battle wagons, waterfalls smoking.
Glaciers two thousand feet deep, in pale blue ice
Wait at violent crags; and avalanches
Fall in white smoke, amongst uprooted trees.
High rock tonnage tilts, before a massed bombardment.

AT HOME IN SINGAPORE

Sometimes I walk down from my nephew's house
In the cool morning, to get some exercise,
Past the Prime Minister's fine mansion,
In Singapore and speak to the Gurkha sentries
Standing fresh and alert at the gates. "Good morning!"
I call to them — "good morning!" they reply.
"And how is the Prime Minister today?"
"Very well, indeed, thank you", they answer me
In lively spirits, and I return the same
With my equatorial smile. 'I am delighted
To hear it!' I say, and continue on my way,
With these cheerful and satisfying exchanges
Resounding in my ears. I find them good
For the digestive well-being of the day.

Singapore 1994

GETTING LOST ROUND US

Stalbridge and Henstridge lead to Templecombe,
Horsington and Stour Provost and Todber,
Compton Pauncefoot, Upton Noble, Gasper
Shepton Montague and Stourton Caundle,
And Wyke Champflower is near Hornblotton Green,
Queen Camel, Chilton Cantelo and Ditcheat,
Fiddleford and Penselwood and Bugley
And Fifehead Magdalen. We are surrounded!
Secrets are set in ancient brick and stone,
Succulent meals remembered, well washed down.
Down through the Deverills, of course, to Mere
There are excitements following the Stour.
Some who get lost between lost Cucklington
And Buckhorn Weston, even disappear.

Wiltshire 1995

CATERINA LAITY

Caterina Laity — beautiful name
For a half-Italian girl, with Cornish husband,
She married down near Truro, where Laity
Is a name well known to people there, I've found.
I met her the other day, in Somerset,
Working at a superstore, with her name
Pinned to her jacket — the perfect ornament.
And I kept saying it over to myself
In the sunshine. It makes a lilt, a carol —
Caterina Laity! — a little dance
Of rhythm for a slender, lively lady —
A line of smiling grace that sums her up
In femininity. There is a something
In laity, too, that sings for pretty folk.

Somerset

CITY OF DREAM

I dreamed, last night, in virtual reality.
I was driving along in an avenue of trees,
Looking across a city in the sun,
To a harbour fine and widespread, filled with liners.
Great funnels like department stores reared up,
Grandly, in rows, and towered with glowing colours,
Against blue sky, and linked the Empire World —
Yellow, red, blue — all colours and devices,
Linking India, Africa, Australia, China,
Canada, Huge battleship stacks of grey,
Massive gleaming funnels, under great masts,
Were thrusting aloft, over upper works, white ensigns —
Part of our Navy — the world's most powerful.
That dream was Southampton, sixty years ago.

DESECRATION, SPITE AND VAINGLORY

Monmouth can be a very crowded town,
With everybody hurrying into Wales,
Or hurrying out again. But here they stay,
And shop around, and all the country folk
Come busily in as well, from all about,
To eat and buy and sell and sit and drink,
With the free parking in the Old Market, there.
And there is a sign in handsome Agincourt Square,
Pointing to Monmouth Castle, up the hill,
Where Henry the Fifth was born, son of Bolingbroke.
Although Cromwell slighted it, with angry spite,
He couldn't pull down our Agincourt, nor make
His Tumbledown Dick continue base destruction.
Spite and hatred will never rule England long.

THE HOCKEY I FORGOT — (BUT ORDERS ARE ORDERS)

I used to play rugger at school, and on
My training ship, HMS *Worcester*, but
Was always getting hurt, so I tried hockey,
At which I was rather safer, and I took
It up again, after the war — very rusty.
I joined a good team, to play against the town.
It was mixed and dangerous, the girls were tough.
"You'll be a Back", our Captain said to me.
"What do I do?" — "Oh just stand in the way,
When their forwards attack." So when a large
Sixteen stone fellow came racing down to our goal,
I stood in his way and cracked two ribs on the butt
Of his stick, and he lay stunned, a bit. "He just
Stood in my way!" moaned the fallen medical student.

THE YOBS OF SPRING

The blackbird and the thrush in sunny trees,
The little pretty birds, much lower down
        Start shouting in the Spring
        With loud and tuneful ease
        And ownership and pride
While collared doves go oohing round the town.
        But sparrows have no need to sing
        Or fuss about their territories,
        They get in lady blackbird's bath
        Although she threatens them.
        They push bold robin to one side
            Who stands up in their path,
        Raiding his crumbs and everything —
            Yobs without fear or shame.

SMALL RIVER SONG

Small river quickens down from the high moors,
The rivulets in its clear, hurrying surface
Under leaves and sky, moving, dividing,
With glittering tendrils, breaking up against
Pale and dark stones — threading bright-cut, bubbling —
Joining, returning to unbroken mirrors
Of pools, that fish-leap and mayfly ring and break.
It reflects the bridge, in the sun again, alight;
It grows in propelling, quickening change.
The river presses under melting boulders,
Still musically fine, through woodland fern.
It has distant singing, purity of passage —
A hushing harpsichord, a moonlit message
That brings on sleep, where pillowed worries turn.

SONNET FOR A BLACKBIRD

The blackbird's voice spills into sunlight
        As the cloud opens its high wing.
Unrehearsed in beauty, purely fresh,
He shouts out phrases true as the young Spring,
Sweet-different, and stops as suddenly.
Then a long set of variations — free
        Fall, like the dew —
In the freshet pride of them, all new,
        And proud as the first few ...
Hypnotic gilt-rimmed eye in glassy view,
Aggressive head and gold beak too,
        And burnished like a banker's shoe —
        He hurries away along the wall,
Firmly in silence, having delivered all.

LIFE ABSOLUTE

What is our life? It is the little shadow
Which runs over the Plain and vanishes
Into the sunset, where those worshippers
Of Stonehenge sun — those chanters of old prayers
Once lived, under a consciousness of stars,
On this globe (shown flat-relative by Mercator)
        Under our absolute above.
I feel a summer in a golden spring —
Life coming across the grass of everything,
        In the great absolute of Love —
Forgiving love, thrice relative Creator.
New life's Son — New Adam, rather,
Through the Mother, from our Father
Brings life's absolute and perfect measure.

LIVING WITH BIRDS

Birds open their arms for feathered propulsion,
Waterproof and warm, when they take food
From beauty's egg, and go into the sky
To become great aeronauts around the world —
High, accurate navigators, night and day,
Skilled in nest building and finding all their needs.
Though they cross oceans and continents,
They still survive, in spite of all, on landing.
They are fine at singing and protecting their young,
But are defenceless against humanity,
Nor can they save us — even from ourselves.
Because these creatures are being uncreated
By us — the sapient species — great and small,
If they fly to extinction, they will take us all.

YOUNG LOVER'S HONEY POT

The young beauty allows long looking to you,
She joins your desire and maintains indifference.
She moves the profile of her body and moistens
The excitement of her lips. She turns a little
To show a little — she knows what your desire is.
Your desire is for her, and her desire
Is for this desire of yours and she will build it
Up in you and never say a word.
And this matter has put you on fire, she knows it.
She will pass the time of day with her lips
Smiling, and her eyes gentle — if you excite her;
Before you can reply, she has added you up.
You've put yourself into her honeypot
And it's no good trying to struggle out of it.

CARTMEL RACES (THE WINNING ORDER)

We were all distressed by the wrapped flag
At the Grand National start. In fact the race
Turned out to be a disaster for the nation.
They order things much better down in Cartmel.
After a race there, recently, the judge
Altered the order (and the rules as well).
For close finishes he holds up his stick
Vertically before him, for the first nose
Past it. But after this race he found his stick
Had warped (left out in the rain overnight).
He is a decisive man, of monumental
Probity, and, sensing the injustice
Of the first decision — indeed, the bent result,
He changed the order, and nobody complained.

WET WEATHER ROSES — WILTSHIRE

Wet weather roses, melting yellow yolk
And deep pink pleasure, dripping, drooping,
Dropping down, no sun of life — gold lamp,
To light their pride, restore their grouping,
To draw their scent and beauty up the stalk.
With bee and butterfly, no nodding play,
Day after day they stay in a cold swamp;
Wasting their colour and all of their shape away.
Flakes of sugar melting on the ground,
Spilling on the leeched earth, without a sound;
Without a gold reflection,
Gusted to wet destruction,
With shiver in the trees. Goodbye! Sweet roses,
Never to display breathtaking poses.

DOWN TO THE FALKLANDS TO SCRATCH A WHALE

In the nineteen thirties our ship would head
Down south through the Atlantic, to get the wool
From the Falkland Islands, and calling at
Gran Canaria and the Cape Verde Islands,
Ascension, St. Helena and passing Tristan.
There were thousands of tons to be collected
At Port Stanley, and a lot of cargo,
To be delivered there — supplies much needed.
A great whale (I think Old Bill) would meet us,
Miles outside Port Stanley and escort
Us in. How he knew we were coming, no one
Could explain. He did a lot of scratching
Along our ship's side, as we were entering.
Then we went home through the Straits of Magellan.

IN THE STRAITS OF MAGELLAN

In the Straits of Magellan we often called
At Punta Arenas and anchored just outside
The harbour. Nearby there was another ship —
Almost a hulk, really, at anchor there.
It was a fine, historic relic of ours.
It may have been called *The "Great Britain"*, say, or some
Such name as that, and we were sorry for it,
And lowered a boat and went to look at it.
We were young trainee officers, we climbed
Up the deserted ship's side, on a rope ladder,
Left hanging down to the water, sixty years
Ago. We explored it and carved our names,
All three of us, into the woodwork, there.
The ship was built of iron — one of the first.

NAVIGATOR 1940. *For Maureen Dufferin*

Clandeboye! I loved that great stylish house,
With the musical name, to return to,
During the war. I have often dreamed of it.
My ship was HMS *Widgeon*, powering back
To Belfast and the docks, through the wide lough,
At night, and rounding dark Donaghadee,
That coast half seen — it was like thinking of home —
After hard days at sea, patrolling danger.
And when we left for Dunkirk the owner lined up
All the staff, with her butler heading them —
Two friendly lines, to wish safe navigation.
The dark woods and the lake, and the grey house,
Beautifully ruling its surroundings —
Peace was there — pale beautiful ruling lady.

NORTHERN PATROL — HMS *NORTHERN PRINCESS* 1941
Account of a hurricane

In the war we patrolled below the Arctic —
Where night was day, in the mad midnight sun —
Ten miles apart in case the enemy's
Pocket battleships broke out into the Atlantic.
We rolled funnel under, in those heavy seas,
Because our ships were not designed for war.
They had been built as fast whale-oil vessels,
With powerful reciprocating steam
Engines, and low pressure turbines aft of them
On the twin shafts, to give them extra speed,
From the same economical use of steam.
They were larger and more powerful than trawlers,
And like them, very storm-worthily built, and strong,
With good stability — till they were altered.
They brought the whale oil home before the last war
From the factory ships out in the Arctic,
Into Port Sunlight, at speed, through violent weather.
Their holds carried a heavy tonnage of oil
In barrels. There were twelve of them, brand new,
Which the Navy had arranged to commandeer,
Pre-war, from Lever Brothers, to arm and convert,
For the Northern Patrol — the Admiralty's eyes, there.
But with no cargo below — just a big crew,
(About forty officers and men, all told)
And much top-hamper needed for warships,
They were top-heavy and unstable in storm.
With guns fitted high, to make them useful,
And insufficient counter-ballasting,
There was storm-danger if the engines broke down.
My Captain was Lieutenant-Commander Hulse.
We were well equipped for anti-submarine work,
However, with some modern electronics.
For enemy battleships we had great masts,
That could send powerful radio signals
To report the sighting of big ships breaking out
Into the Atlantic against our convoys —
We could signal Whitehall and Admiralty.
For they would have to pass through our patrol lines

Up there, against the Arctic — our watchful presence,
And if one did so, we had every chance
To make a quick battleship report, before
They banged us into oblivion, with their guns.

Just to fall into the sea was death, there,
From the savage degrees of cold — the rigging iced up,
Frozen sea water constantly coming aboard.
So we patrolled and froze and searched grey seas,
Rolling near upside down, to funnel under,
With a dreadful wait, before she righted herself.
Some of the worst weather in the world begins there,
In that area, above and around Iceland.
When storms occur, they can be hurricanes.
One day (actually night!) we met one
While our turbine engines were broken down
And useless — the Chief Engineer reported
That the main bearings had run — near seized, so
A lot of our power was gone, when the slamming began.
We were a paper boat in a liquidiser.
The wall of wind bringing the water, broke
Over us in a tunnel of thunder-buckling tonnage
Upon us, from waves, sixty feet high above us,
Seemingly joined together and whizzing around.
Everything — even rivetted to the deck — went over
The side, and we lay on our beam ends, smashed.
We were in confused troughs, pressed over, and held down,
With much sea down our funnel, into the engines,
We could no longer turn into the wind.
We were bound to break silence for a "Mayday"
Signal, because, enemy or not, we were sinking
Anyway. So we fired signal rockets
As we lay in confused troughs of bellowing seas.
Our sister ship sighted them, and laboured
Towards us, from ten miles away, most bravely.
Instead of riding out, head-to-sea, for safety,
She struggled to our aid, and kept down wind,
In case she blew into us. I was First Lieutenant.
My captain was shouting out from the bridge to me,
As I prepared for a tow, having rigged lines
For safety, for the crew to hold to, in deep seas
Coming aboard. We had to rig a great rope

(A medium hawser) for towing — along the ship's side —
Shouting orders, when nothing could be heard —
Half the time underwater — tying it outside
Everything, in the way — or the resultant
Strain between ships, would rip everything down.
The Captain shouted against the wind "Number one!"
(To me) — "Secure everything outboard, and beyond-all..."
"Ay ay sir!" (I was doing it) but he couldn't see me.
He struggled down to me, at last, satisfied.

Our sister ship was firing Schermuly rockets
At us, in the shrieking night-day, they
Carried a strong wire line to fall across us,
But the wind was blowing their rockets back
Out of the sky at them! My captain signalled
"Go round to the windward and chance it!"... and they did!
(He was the senior captain of Northern Patrol).
It gave them desperate struggle as we hung on —
Frequently they disappeared in the huge troughs,
But *with* the wind's blast the powerful rockets
Blew *across* our ship, with their rocket lines.
We secured them to our intermediate rope,
Tied and stretched double the length of our ship's side,
With small cord lashings to give way when tugged,
In this battering hurricane — so that our rescue
Ship could haul it on board them, and then bend it
To their vast Insurance Hawser; and we
Could winch it back to us, and shackle it
To our anchor chain, from which we'd removed
And stopped-off a bow anchor. "Are we set?"
I shouted to Mr Pegler's ear — he nodded —
(My Hebridean Warrant Officer)
All went well — the Intermediate tore, whipping
And cracking away from the length of our hull —
Our waterlogged ship's side — and then fell clear,
With a cheer as our rescuers winched it in —
Standing off well away from us, dipping and hidden
In the grey frenzy. We lay there, half-wrecked,
Battered by mad, high, runaway monsters
In screeching inferno, doing duties
With all our strength, which were normally easy,
And being knocked down and crushed by great sea-walls.

We never lost anybody overboard, thank God!
Though a number of men half drowned on deck,
In the scuppers. Our Captain still manoeuvred
Main engines skilfully, to keep well away
From our sister ship, and disaster of collision,
Without the use of seized-up turbine engines.
Heaven knows what went, with sea in the engine room —
If anything parted now, we were done!
Everything was deafening, everything strummed
And screamed — ropes screamed — plates buckled badly,
Lifeboats went overboard in splintered chunks.
Our forward armoured gun-shield was crumpled round
Its gun, by the tonnage of a wave-blow —
Each sixty feet high, and several hundred tons,
Hurled down the ship's length by a wall of wind;
The steel — a grey wrapping-paper — with ice —
Enclosing its gun, in a burst grey parcel.
Thank heavens the steam pipes to our winches worked,
As we began the heavy hauling over
From our rescue ship, of their huge hawser —
A great wire rope; woven as thick as your thigh,
Enormous Anaconda — a steel cable —
Which gradually, in a great bight, inched in
Towards us, brought by our hauling rope, wrapped round
Our winch still. Soon the vast snake's eye appeared,
And climbed inboard to reach our waiting men,
On the diving fo'c'sle, half buried down a trough,
With frozen beards, and fingers still alert, there,
At the anchor chain. They quickly shackled it
To the ice-bound waiting link, as the ship staggered
And plunged down heavily, under precipitous sea.
Nobody lost any fingers in that effort! —
Fingers, or a limb ... lives ... easily lost there!
Men have been cut in half by snapping steel hawsers.
I had a fine ship's company — well trained
And long experienced in bitter sea-war —
For sudden emergent dangers, complications,
Not only for a battle, but in the great
Trawler seamanship which they exercised.
Some of my best men were Hebridean,
Nothing appalled them — They were fishermen!
Limpets on rocks! — They clung in raving waves.
Their singing accents rang out clear and calm.

And they simply got to work with a hurricane,
Lashing things down, and holding the ship together
A quiet rugger team, scoring a try.
Anyone watching this crew's deliberate actions
Would scarcely guess how perilous the battle!
And I thanked God that we had all survived it —
So busy we'd no time beyond the urgent,
To see how dreadful the escape had been.
I was grateful for the Lever-built strength
Of the hull, with my grip on the safety line
We had rigged — watching the giant hawser
With the iced catenary of its own weight,
Between the two ships — near an eighth of a mile
In length, absorbing titanic forces!
As one ship blasted up, the other dived down,
And disappeared in a valley, altogether.
Then the tow began, after we signalled "ready".

Once we headed into the sea, we rode much better.
The hurricane lessened to storm, and then died down.
Then began a thousand mile tow to Scotland —
To Aberdeen, and very extensive repairs.
We left a big gap in patrol defences —
Twenty miles wide, at least, for a battleship!
Luckily we had survived disaster,
And luckily no battleship went through.
Afterwards *Northern Princess* was lost on patrol,
In the cold sea sunk, with Pegler and McGinnis,
And all my comradely, trained, ship's company,
And the new C.O. who took the ship over from me.
And amongst them all was lost the Scottish gypsy,
I had taken out on our rabbiting days in Orkney,
To give him lost country freedom for a spell —
The gentle lad with the ferret, was gone as well.

THE PINNACLES OF JOYOUS GARDE

The shapely rocks that tower above Fair Island
Rise vertical, straight out of the blue sea.
On Northern Patrol we used to make a call there,
Looking for enemy submarines or landings,
Under those rocketing steeples of sharp beauty,
They rear straight upward into fine blue sky,
Pearl grey, lit by the sun. We fired our guns
At them, because our Captain wondered whether
A four inch shell, or shells, could topple down
A storm-carved turret, but the answer is no,
Or else our target-practice from several miles
Away, was very poor. They did no damage.
We were made less, by this failed vandalism,
Bombarding the pinnacles of Joyous Garde.

Fair Isle 1941

"SUNK AT ONCE"

I was spare C.O. at R.N. Barracks,
Where some days could be idle now and then.
So three of us, a surgeon lieutenant
(Whose idea it was) a midshipman,
And myself, used to get up early to swim
In the Barracks' covered Swimming Bath,
Before seven, for some healthy exercise.
One morning we found that the high diving board
Was broken and there was steel scaffolding there.
Determined to be clever, I climbed up
To near the high ceiling, and then inched along
The scaffolding, to dive from the middle, when
The caging collapsed and fell somersaulting down.
I broke my neck and blood came out of my ears.
The others stayed up holding on to the ropes.

The surgeon lieutenant was an able fellow,
And reckoning something was wrong, dropped down
To the water, beside me, and phoned up
The Barracks Ambulance. I was not conscious.
Nobody could wake me at the hospital.
I was in a coma, my father was sent for;
He had a command in Plymouth, and came over
When he could. After some days they were ready
Almost, to box me up, when they decided
Blood was pressing on my brain, in the spinal
Column. So they gave me a lumbar puncture,
With my father present and I came round
In a flash, and said "hallo!" to them all —
And very surprised at the fuss. "What's going on?"

I had annoyed and worried a lot of people,
Including the Commodore of R.N. Barracks,
Who had just arranged an appointment for me —
HMS *Empire Audacity* was a new ship,
In more ways than one — a new departure —
A "Woolworth Carrier" — the first of its kind,
And a great idea of Winston Churchill's for
Defence of Atlantic Convoys. But it was
A bit expendable, as were its planes.
It had a rudimentary flight deck,
And some guns, and was intended for
The menace of the wolf-pack submarines,
That were sinking so many of our ships.
Now I should have to miss the chance for glory.
The appointment would have to go to someone else.
Later, when I recovered, at my request,
I was sent to the Mediterranean
Where war was getting busy. We had to go round
Africa, as the enemy blocked the Med,
To troopships. I took part in an exhibition
Bout, of boxing, to amuse the troops,
With an R.A.F. P.T. Instructor.
It was the big Dutch troopship, *Nieuw Amsterdam*,
Converted from a fast liner, in our Yards;
Carrying thousands of our army men,
Mostly, and we had been a week at sea.
We travelled without convoy at high speed.
That night, naval officers were asked to join

In watch-keeping duties, on the bridge, to help
The ship's complement, in dangerous waters.
I was with an angry Welsh officer.
He said "I've got no kit — *nothing at all!* —
Why? — I've lost it all! I was given a ship
At the last moment — *Empire Audacity* —
Some fool broke his neck, and I took over .. *sunk!*
Only myself, and a few others survived! —
Sunk at once! ... well .. not long out of *bloody harbour!*"

A VAN DELIVERY *c.*1955

I remember the great Marquess of Bath
Sliding a big tray of small pottery figures
Out of the back of his van, in Cheddar,
With his young son helping, as they delivered
A batch of them, all breakables, to their shop,
At the entrance of the Caves. I can see them
Now, a photographic study of care,
And concentration, of two working people,
Carrying them — the profile of a man —
And a handsome man at that — rugged and strong
There was no mistaking that nose of his, at all,
Nor that proud and understanding purpose,
With droll good humour, under serious cover.
He was known, and very much liked, by folk around here.

FOR ANGELA

Angela has always had some look,
For us, of Ingrid Bergman — the fine structure
In her face and eyes — the pride of cheekbone —
A beautiful woman out of tragedy ...
Her husband, Count von Friedensberg surrendered
The shadow of Austria to the Russians —
And a whole horrifying reign of terror.
He had no option, of course, and was the only
General the Russians would accept,
Being of the old school, and a good soldier.
The Russians should know, for they were very thorough
In sorting out, then, many for just revenge,
In the Stalinism of a common ruin.
But she's true Mozart music — smiling in shadow.

GREAT THRILLING BETTERWARE CUP CHASE
(3 miles 110 yards) *1.55 Ascot 16th December 1995*

So many great horses fell in a field of nine!
Richard Dunwoody rode Unguided Missile —
Great Woody with a good plan, keeping well back,
On the long Chase, nurtured his mount at the jumps,
While others fell — Young Hustler, Couldn't Be Better,
Then Riverside Boy and Yorkshire Gale — all went.
But Woody was watching Rough Quest, and soon the duel
Began! — When he drew clear of Unholy Alliance,
With Jamie Osborne — that stylish, brilliant rider.
There was a mistake at one of the last fences,
But Woody was ready, and picked the Missile up —
And again! — off his nose! and fought for and caught
Rough Quest!
Who ran out of line a bit, with Mick Fitzgerald.
Then they went at it! and Woody won by a neck!

ON THE BORDER

I said to the old man who does the garden,
Of the Red Lion in Bredwardine — "my friend
How do you pronounce the name of this village —
Is it dyne or deene?" "I don't know, boy,"
He said, "I come from Wales." I looked across
The quiet woods, up the road, beyond the hill —
"That's Wales", I agreed (standing in Herefordshire)
"That's right" — with a proud, far-away expression.
His voice was border music, in the soft tones.
He had come his five or six miles to work,
From his cottage, and was going home
To his own country. "I'll be seeing you then."
And he went back to his Principality,
Up the road. His talk was all a lilting song.

ARMED THIEF ON THE *MARABISHI MARU*. 1936

Our motorship, *La Paz*, was in Callao harbour
Peru, and it was a bright fine day there,
And rattling busy too, in the docks. Alongside
Was a rare Japanese ship, unloading cargo.
Down their gangway, right in front of me,
As I came up on deck, stumbled an hombre,
In white shirt, black knife-sash, blue trousers.
He seemed half-crouching drunk, but at the foot
Facing me, he turned and fell, face down.
On the back of his shirt spread a red stain,
From which the point of the long knife they carried
Was sticking out. He had tried to rob a cabin,
I heard, but the Jap officer was inside it,
And with a swift movement, gave his knife back to him.

THE ENCHANTED CITY

I seek the forgotten city of Trebizond —
Holy walled bastion of gold and glory,
That ruled Byzantium, and held the gate
Of Christian Empire in the Black Sea, alone,
For the last decade of Grecian Palaces,
Pillared high over a blue peacock harbour.
I'll raise that half demolished City-State —
Monastic beauty, mansions with vine and arbour,
And in massed lantern-glare, see mounted there,
The Imperial Guards again! With trumpet calls,
We'll wake the golden façades, the fortress walls! —
Basilicas of the Black Sea, shine bright!
Fanfares Augustan! — Blind Homer's voice beyond!
Call up the down-fallen Towers of Trebizond!

THE CHURN OWL

It's time, I think, to hear the Churn-owl's call,
Again, as the days blossom, and the nights
Grow warm, and the first months that froze us all,
Were swallowed up in April's melting sights —
The cold grip on us, prettily undone.
The butterflies persuade their wings to dry,
And early sun brings out the silly fly,
That stays alert until the shine has gone,
And joins in woodland gangs to dance away
The evening light, under the Churn-owl's bough,
And his approving eye (or, as some say) —
The Nightjar, flown from Africa, just now.
He studies them, then opens his great gape
And swoops down on them all, and few escape.

ARANJUEZ

Spanish place names that harangue the mind!
With grandeur of old palaces in the rain,
War chargers, progress of ancient stateliness,
The continent past of all magnificence —
Segovia, Toledo and Sevilla!
Gold battlements, treasured glory of dark lemon
Trees, dark song of guitars, harp hungriness,
Trumpets for the fading façades of Time!
They spread along arboreal boulevards —
Call across vehicular avenues
Of shoppers, of palms, to courtyards of ancient music.
They fill a towering bellwork, imperial mullions,
And arabesques. Trumpets of pillared arcades
Harangue me! — Aranjuez! — Aranjuez de Castilla!

STEEPLECHASE

Here's the steeplechase care and clash and thunder of winning!
The urgent sound of leather and bridled speed —
Athletic endeavour, still greedy at good ground —
Horse and rider trained to gain the lead,
And between-the-ears excitement at the sight
Of that great fence — the water jump — arriving!
Wind rush, rhythm, control on the right foot,
And well together for take-off spot and spacing,
Perfectly executed — in the air — !...
Over the last fence, leading — good height and neatly
Down! — full throttle — go now! — but with a careful,
Quick glance back, to see immediate challenge —
Head down, streamlined in the stirrups — green turf to the post,
With the final fence behind you, and great achievement!

THE LOSS OF THE *NORTHERN PRINCESS*

We anchored at Kirkwall in Orkney, sometimes
After patrol, or moored alongside the jetty,
With another of our force, in the Northern Patrol —
Which consisted of a flotilla. Our ships
Were smart in appearance, considering the weeks
At sea, in Iceland weather, and all the ships'
Companies were glad to be free on land,
In the old town, with ancient shops and pubs.
It was a full, busy Naval harbour there,
Seldom seen by people back in England.
The smaller warships ranged along the jetty.
The grey old town crumbled up its wind-blown street,
Into the hills behind; over the harbour;

Or lingered about the harbour, here and there.
The enormous edifice of St Magnus Cathedral
Appeared (seen from the sea) out of proportion,
And overturning the island into the water —
Sitting on the edge, with an overbalance,
Joined by the Castle — two enormous frogs
On a water-lily leaf — very top-heavy.
The protected wide waters of Scapa Flow —
Molten polish of great anchorage water,
Held every size of warship, spread about
Distantly, towards surrounding islands;
And the First War German Fleet lay rusting below.
We sometimes went over to the far big ships,
And I went to HMS *Hood*, only just before
She pursued *Bismarck* and met sudden disaster.
Little did anyone, making motor boat calls
To that motionless mass, think of her as destroyed —
Soon to be burst open, torn apart, and sunk! —
By plunging long range gunfire from *Bismarck*!
Green trees were not encouraged by the winds
And the high hills, bald as a green snooker ball.
We were always looking for extra food to buy —
Small goodies in the grocer, biscuits and cheese,
Fresh eggs and marmalade, Marmite and toffee,
And other items for cheering long patrols.
Fresh vegetables, were flown in by our friend
In the R.A.F., from Scotland, in an old bomber —
"The Flying Greengrocer", who came on board us
For drinks in the wardroom, from time to time —
A disabled pilot, getting war-earned rest,
A tall young man — tired eyes, bad liver trouble.
Our troops looked for fresh meat, which was quite scarce,
But luckily the farmers had a plague
Of rabbits on their land, and we were asked
To help reduce the numbers, when in harbour.
I spoke to my men about a hunt in the hills —
We had a wonderful set of Scottish sailors
From the Islands and Highlands and the cities —
Strong quiet folk, except in time of pleasure,
Signed on for the war, including Hebridean
Fishermen from Stornoway, and parts
Remoter still. There was a young Scottish Gypsy

From the wide Highland area, whose home
Tended to move about a lot, under
The wide sky. He owned a ferret, which was our mascot.
We had been offered "a very good breakfast"
By the farmer I met, and his family, above us,
Sheltering in the windy and bare slopes —
Friendly, fine people, They urged us to come,
And, of course, our men were keen. I promised
To bring a party of fifteen of them,
Including our gypsy lad, whose name I forget.
But I remember that his ferret was called
Of all names "Montmorency". It was his pet,
Which I'd given him leave to keep on board.
It was very well behaved, and a good sailor.
But I don't know how it came by its name.
I arranged we should leave the ship before dawn
With bacon sandwiches and flasks of tea
And some long poles for bringing back our catch,
Because we hoped to give some of the bag
To a sister ship of ours, moored alongside.
We wore a varied assortment of working gear
For rabbiting — "dog-robbers" rig for all —
A wicked set of villains in the dark —
All animated faces — craggy, or round,
Weathered men. They were a family team,
With close-knit dignity and discipline,
Even in enjoyment. But they were men.
They had a nucleus of trawler discipline.
To know them, you had to sit amongst them,
Not just in a pub, but at a good meal,
And join the animated, carved faces,
Their conversation, out of the solid oak —
As they faced one another across a table,
Eating, drinking, joking at a spread —
Scottish people with good table behaviour.
They were a strong company of related warmth —
Some weaker, but all with known characteristics.
I was having trouble with our gypsy sailor.
He was an excellent seaman, very willing,
But troublesome to the rest. It was his habit —
Some psychological stress — to wet his bunk

At night — giving offence to all in the fo'c'sle,
Even when he readily slung a hammock,
Instead. I believe he lived an imprisonment,
On board a ship, for a long time, surrounded.
In confined living quarters, he gave offence, there.
I was quietly arranging to get him put ashore,
For the men's comfort and his own freedom.
Young Naval medical men took less persuading,
And this solution was agreed. But senior
Old salts (brought back) ashore could be difficult —
Snortingly difficult to persuade, in wartime,
When there was need for men to stay at sea.
The comfort of a ship's company seemed less
To men ashore, discussing "the ship's fighting
Efficiency" — which was my point as well! —
Fighting men's comfort! — But we were busy, now,
Reaching the high, bare, rabbit-swarming fields,
With burrows everywhere, they were overrun.
The hill we chose, seemed to be one whole warren.
Rabbits were all about, and almost tame.
The young Scot, the gypsy, was very quick
At setting his nets, and putting in Montmorency.
He caught the rabbits at once, and then I noticed
He didn't want to kill. I had to take over,
Though I didn't care for it, either, on that scale,
And I dealt with it somewhat unwillingly.
But I gave each one a sharp chop with the side
Of my hand, behind the head — held by the hind
Legs — as I had learned from my grandfather's
Men, in Devon, as a boy, on such excursions.
Some of the other seamen helped me, too,
After watching; and we soon had gained —
Far quicker than anyone had expected —
A big bag, to take down, which the gypsy seaman
Arranged along our poles — brace after brace.
We were a cheerful party in the hills.
We'd eaten our sandwiches first, at the first light,
And drunk our tea and coffee, and had caught
Full forty brace — with a lot of exercise
Chasing escapees, there were so many.
By nine-thirty in the morning, we were down
At the farm gates, with raving appetites,
Ready to attack two breakfasts. Several agreed

They could start "with a full sack of potatoes"
As a foundation for their stomach needs.
In the big farm kitchen, round the scrubbed table,
We sat down amazed at the provisions,
Beside a wide peat fire of roaring brightness.
There was no rationing on Orkney farms!
There was honey in great combs and butter
Freshly made. There were new Orcadian
Loaves, dishes sizzling up with crisp, cured bacon,
Farm sausages, eggs by the dozen, fried
Potatoes (they forgot the sack they'd discussed,
When coming down the hill) — their cavernous hunger
So fully rewarded, here, with much besides,
As well, and plenty of extra helpings.
The breakfast was gigantic! a great meal!
I can see them all, sitting around that table —
The laughter, the cheerful eyes, the full enjoyment
Of hunger satisfied, after dawn efforts
In the fields overhead. It was a great time.
The farmer's wife had come in, looking around
To make sure we were well supplied, and puzzled —
Asked for the officer in charge — and amused
At the comradely gusto. She couldn't pick me out
From the rest, and I smiled up, as she passed me,
With grateful thanks, and said I would stay there —
That it was fine. She wanted me to go
Into her dining room, but she understood
That I was better placed with my ship's people,
And let me be. I shall always remember that meal.
It seemed to me very like being part of a Clan.
One after another they pushed back their chairs
Or rested their elbows, in a cleared space to chat.
It is an oil painting, an Old Master;
You can see the brush strokes, the technique,
In the rich fire-lit brown, each jutting question,
Facial expression, response, highlights and eyes.
Autumn in the morning — kitchen breakfast,
Spread and scattered across grained, kitchen table.
There's lively argument and solid comfort;
There's open mouths (and a good deal of "stuffing")
There's light on half-empty plates, and more passed down.
There's buzz and clatter, deep laughter, quiet feeding,

The sitting back, of replete content, with teacups.
It was the last time I saw them so, together,
In the morning of their good company.
Mr Pegler, the small mahogany man
Of deeds, and Tarbert, McGregor and McManus
McGillivray, Urquhart, Kilbride and the gypsy,
And the absent others — all forty fighting men,
Leading seamen, able — ordinary none!
There never was a story of more woe...
Men battling with the savage Polar ocean,
And by it's grey, hooded armies, overwhelmed.

When we came down the long winding street
Into Kirkwall and along to our jetty —
The long stone jetty, with a number of warships
Moored alongside, we certainly got attention,
With our lengthy poles, weighted with dangling rabbits,
Brace after brace of them, bending the wood.
We swaggered like a gang of successful poachers —
Very popular, as we strode through the harbour —
Sixteen of us, in all, with eighty rabbits.
Sailors caught sight of us and came ashore,
Begging for a few rabbits for the pot,
And we had to make a judgement, justly.
But we all did well. Rabbit in cider!
I haven't a doubt was the favourite menu.
The gypsy sailor was well considered, too.
And so was Montmorency, that agent,
Under ground, a very productive mascot —
For the ship, lucky — lucky for a while.

I remember that particular outing well —
Everything was drawing to an end —
Because the next night I had been invited
To the Argyll and Sutherland Highlanders' Ball,
With other Naval officer friends who had
A few days leave from the Arctic Patrol.
I had reported to Base, adversely, about
Our engines — never properly repaired.
By then, *Northern Princess* had twice been towed.
And I put in a last word on behalf
Of the gypsy, to free him from his prison.
I was handing my ship over, and leaving.

Sadly our friends in the Highland regiment,
Were leaving the island, too, altogether,
For some urgent war service, far away.
This dance was their lively last one. They called it,
In honour of the famous fighter plane —
"The Spitfire Ball", and they held an auction
For contributions to their Spitfire Fund,
And included the sale of a beagle hound,
From their famous pack, which was breaking up.
And I bought him, as I was leaving, too,
Soon after. My Captain had long left, and I
Was in command, until a new C.O.
And First Lieutenant arrived. So I was busy.
I handed over. It was my turn to go,
And I made the long journey home, to R.N. Barracks
In Plymouth, having said goodbye to the men.
And *Northern Princess* went out on her last patrol
Into radio silence, and sank alone.

HUNT BALL

And now tell me
Where pretty maids can be
That once were all in a row —
The lithe, divine, curvaceous maid
I would have by my side —
Proud to be squire and guide
And dance with her knee to knee,
In love's fine steeplechasing ride.
And if she would or no
Was small beside
The embracing pride
The musical escapade,
The breathless point-to-point of getting-to-know.
And so to couple and a whirling go!

SWEET FANCY'S ELEGY
(Variation on a theme)

Wind in roadside bramble shrieks
        Starving crow on thorn.
    Grass whistle, bough that creaks,
        And a wrecked sky —
So where does warm-lipped Fancy lie? —
        With a pebble for an eye,
        Underneath! underneath!
        In the cold forlorn.

Nobody lives — or loves the heath.
        Here are empty hills
        Of barren poverty.
        See! — see!
    Everything has blown away!
    Here lies place of dreadful ills,
        Gravel-grey the day,
    And a stone for Fancy's pay.

THE BARBADOS SHOATS

Oliver Messel came to the Museum
One day, and I met him under the great archway.
"Hallo Mr Maycock, have you been away
Out of the Island?" "No", I replied,
"I've been over to Maycock town, in St Lucy,
To see how the old place is getting on."
"Did you meet many of your subjects there?"
"Just a few friends", I laughed, "and a lot of sheep —
A big herd of Black-Bellied sheep, quite vocal —
And several gave me rather a funny look,
As well." "Were they trying to tell you something?"
"I'm not sure" I said. "Of course, they're not into
Democracy — it's food with them, not votes.
But they're confusing as sheep, and look like goats".

SHOUTING ABOUT THE SPRING

The sun came out so hot,
So gold and bright,
That I tied it to an April chimney pot
Today,
To stop it going in, and out of sight,
And taking our delight
Away.
Now I can shout and sing
About the sunny Spring —
A lot!

THE DIVINER

"Good morning" said the girl, there,
At the check-out, "Good morning" I said, too.
And I added — "How are you?"
"I'm fine!" she said.
"And I don't know where
I've seen anyone finer!" —
I added warmly, when I'd read
Her face a pretty while —
(Being like a diviner)
But she turned her eyes away —
And then there was a smile
You won't see in a while!

ODE TO CHARLTON PARK
(Adagio ma non troppo)

The most beautiful woman in the world
Is a house, is a palace, with turquoise turrets —
Four, coppered into the sky at the four corners,
The towers of beautiful, lost, Charlton Park.
She stands in the green island of her magic
With some of her cool avenue of trees.
She is the marvel of a lovely woman
Still perfectly enchanting as great music,
Still magically patrician, slender yet full.
And yet she knows defeated ambience —
Sadness of relegation in her long life,
That is Suffolk overcast — even in June.
In shadows astray, she stands in her own loss,
In old green trees, in ripple-shimmer of leaves,
Awaiting restitution to full living ...
The three grim Sisters point and weigh and spin ...
And yet much is still perfect. Loss is there,
But Charlton stands up in her quiet Park
Awaiting entertainment, carriages, cars,
A Summer Ball, wine, poetry and music
Again — the parties, the welcome wheels. But silence
Has come to her leased apartments ... a sad spell ...
A house divided — let to long-term living —
Not lost in Trust, or a dusted museum — she lives
On, so ... and the horses and the dogs remain.
She lives, and that's the best of it, by far —
But in sad heart, reverting to the background.
Charlton's loss is the gain of the Agent's House —
Excellent beauty — the eighteenth century
Informed it; and now full family life — today's
Young family, with Philippa and Tasha
And Alexander, now studying at Oxford.
And there are the grand stables, filled with horses,
That the first Earls built, elegant, and classic —
(This Protestant branch of the Howards) the Earls of Suffolk.
Charlton village is a well-tended heirloom,
Small, fine, unspoiled, of emerald and silver,
In Wiltshire meadows — a jewel of Malmesbury.
There is a lady living in a cottage
There, a tenant for fifty years, a faithful

Living adherent in this evolution
Of the whole, to front new-adamant change —
A sound historian, uncynical, loyal,
A living archive of the Suffolk magic,
And with a kindness for the truth of love
And loss. She has the keys of the church, and tells
The story of the memorial window —
The loss of the young future — still in arms —
The loss of a Howard of bright beauty ...
And the loss of many fallen in the wars.
Charlton is a magnificent fate's portion,
A beauty in waiting, in a dream of waiting,
And a landscaped shadow, Italianate,
A green dress and ashen wall, surrounding all,
Still absolute, inescapable, enchantment.
From the great House, divided, to the proud calm
Of the Agent's House, winged wide, angelic
In elegance of colour and old softness,
Nothing has gone away. But the loss clings
In beauty, under gaze of hungry Time.
Time has attacked her, yet she smiles at him —
In her magnificent defiant beauty
Charlton is my joy. She is perfection,
Because imperfect, as all true beauty is.

June 1996.

Charlton Park, *Charlton*, Wiltshire. Built 1601
The Earl and Countess of Suffolk and Berkshire.

DORSTONE TO ABBEY DORE

I have been to Presteigne, and eaten well
At the Radnorshire Arms; and Kington, I like,
On the Arrow, and Weobley, and that hotel
Where the lower end of the garden is firmly in Wales
And you can't see the join — though I have searched
For it. At Bredwardine you can gaze out
Of the fishing lodge windows at full orchards —
Moon-blossoming to the Wye — night's ghostly stare
Out of a public house, before the dawn!
You can find heaven in rust-red budding woods,
Absorbing the hush of April's evening bells,
Under Black Mountain. In the Golden Valley
Cross over the height and down, beyond Dorstone, where
Shines the oldest Abbey of continuous prayer.

River Dore, Ewyas Harold, April 1996

POETS P.C.

We compose with true scansion, musical beat,
With vocal rhythm and a dancing line,
With a fresh touch and surety of feet,
Never tangled. (False symbols falsely entwine).
Pick us up and we cannot be put down,
We live in all memory and we renew it.
We haven't been got, to be forgotten clown —
All that's not done is for us to do it —
The breath of secret landscape and the clutch
At loves of the heart, invisible to touch,
We set alight — not just computer show-it.
But personal computer's in true poet —
What's put in, and what is carried about
Is beauty at mind's elbow — we bring it out.

THE GATE UNDER THE WORLD
(The Straits of Magellan)

It's a great while since I stood in the wind
Roaring around Fuego — winds that blow
Into The Magellan, down the thinned,
The wide, scarce-forested Straits, through glaciered snow —
Long, long ago!

There's violent space, immensity unspent —
Andean, crag-ridden, an archipelago land,
Trackless, lashed tail of a vast continent —
Rare folk extinguished by quick trigger, and
Gun's ignorant hand.

Espiritu Sancto and The Virgins, grey
At the Atlantic entrance to the great Strait,
Stood massive. The whole world above us, lay —
The seas, the sky, the whole Earth's Polar weight,
On the great South Gate!

From Punta Arenas there is no destination —
Sky-mountains, islands, inlets, where the winds moan
For three hundred miles! — wild man at Desolación,
Under Wandering Albatross, with eyes of stone,
I saw, alone.

At the Pacific Ocean end, an Indian
With a canoe, lost under a mountain wall,
Was fishing — a matchstick Patagonian
In a stick boat — one man and that was all ...
No sea-birds call.

WILD GOOSE

Grey Goose, well known for staying late —
In proud old days, slow to migrate,
And ever ready to come homing back —
Now, late or early, old Greylag has sped
From this crestfallen island's sovereign door,
Surrounded less by sea, than cynical lack.
Rest easy in your dead computered bed,
The Grey Goose lags beside another shore.
From wherever we were free and great,
Peaceful, to prosperous service dedicate —
Hospital, college, care, road, rail and State,
He has called back the esprit, the freedom skeins,
And all his empire nowhere now remains.
'Fear not! the Grey Goose flieth never more!'

THE LAST DAYS OF THE WOOLWORTH EXPRESS

We would hear the call of The Woolworth Express —
Small tank engine, bustling with carriages (two)
Beyond Yeo Wood — the owl-owned kingdom of it —
The farthest limits of our valley at Plumley.
It ran with soft mutters on its passage home
To Lustleigh, from Bovey Tracey, on the branch
Line — lingering steam — pale cotton fluff in trees,
Between Yarner and Bag Tor (seen in the morning)
Or evening's interrogative by the river —
A breathy pipe, toy rattle of iron wheels,
Over seldom encountered rails, through solemn
Wooded country, lost to all but ourselves,
And deer and the ear of a watchful wild —
Our Eden valley, rustled by South West breezes.

A SAD CASE OF POLLUTION

There was a young lady of Scarborough,
Who fell in a barrel of tarborough,
She'd had vodka and gin,
And was dyed black as sin,
So they tipped her right into the harbourough.

(Composed with the help of my Hairdresser —
a young lady from Scarborough.)

GONE AWAY

You can ask for me at the Bell Inn
At Chalford, and if they don't know,
And can't remember ever having seen
My face, and tell you so;
Then you will have been too late.
I shall have passed through the other gate.
And I expect it will be long ago.